I0560495

BIG
BLUE
SOCIETY

FISHTALES AND MAYHEM

Mark Cavanagh
with
Norman Hansen
Brian Cavanagh
William Lally

Copyright © 2025 Mark Cavanagh

All Rights Reserved

This is a work of non-fiction. Names have been changed and certain identifying characteristic altered to protect the innocent, however the lip protrusions are accurate.

No part of this book may be reproduced, or stored in a retrieval system, or transmitted in any form or by any means, electronic, mechanical, photocopying, recording, tattooing, or otherwise, without express written permission of the publisher.

ISBN: 979-8-9994412-0-1

Cover Design by Damonza
Printed in the United States of America

Photos by Mark and Steven Cavanagh unless noted

DEDICATION

For our parents and forebears who never
knew what they were giving rise to.

For our wives who love us and take us back
when we smell like smoked fish.

For our children who inherit the legacy and have to deal with it.

Friendship is a single soul dwelling in two bodies.

Aristotle

*The laughter shared between best guy friends
can heal even the deepest wounds.*

Anon

Acknowledgements

We wish to thank the people who supported the Society over the years: our friends and families, our dealers, treatment providers, and the folks who rented us boats, campsites, houses and gear. A particular shout to Walt Emmons who set us on the right course at Lower Saranac Lake.

We thank our readers for their comments and corrections, especially Bill and Lori Vincent for proofing the manuscript.

Finally, our gratitude goes to our better halves who are in a class all their own: Robin, Theresa, Kathy, Marty, Debbie, Kim, Elaine, Gert, Denise, Ruth, and Mountain Mama.

Request

If this book brings you a smile or a good flashback, please leave a review on the Big Blue Society Amazon book page. We're sure to read it, and it helps others join the Society.

The first forty years of life give us the text; the next thirty supply the commentary.

Schopenhauer

Contents

FOREWORD

THE STORY THAT drags your ass out of bed at 2:30 in the morning and sets your fingers to flying on the keys needs to be told. You are at its mercy, a stick to its fire, and it burns its way from the inside out. The kicker about this story is that we never intended to tell it in the first place.

The Big Blue is a secret Society. Out where no human eyes can see, where the night is truly dark and the dawn a blinding sear, we set the wild man in us free. We never planned to share the secrets with anyone. They were ours alone, and best kept that way.

This Spring, we buried one of our men and something changed. As I knelt before the coffin, scenes went through my mind that were both ridiculous and sublime. We had been friends for over thirty years and shared a lot in the woods when our spirits were as free as those that flow from a jug. I had a Big Blue ball cap with me, faded from sun, stained with bug juice, and I tucked it in beside my buddy, just in case. It was then that the fire caught, and we've been writing by it ever since.

While trying to set this down, there were chapters I could not write. The eldest member of the Blues, Roger Shitfish, taught us about traditional bluegrass music. He said, "Brothers' voices are meant to come together." That is what is happening here. I throw down the lead, my brother Sausage sings the high part, our cousin Lyle slaps along on the bass, and the guy we call "Bobby" adds some twisted harmony.

Men are taking a lot of crap these days for being men, and this narrative will do nothing to further their cause except to let them know that they are not alone. We are just as screwed-up as the next guy, but we love our women, care for our families, and get responsibly wasted. Don't hold us to "correct" standards and you won't be dismayed by the antics of our merry band of men.

When we were young, we were like the buds on a spruce tree. We broke out of the papery skin all bright and green and stretched out like fingers to the sky. We seasoned with time, hardened to the touch, and sharpened with experience. Then the cold got a hold of us, and something changed on the inside. New buds were forming, ready to bust out on their own.

We have 21 sons between us and a crop of grandkids coming along. They love to hear stories about camping and fishing and are itching to go on trips of their own. Someday, they will, and the fire will speak to them as it has to us. Cones are falling, seeds are taking root, and the future is clear: the Big Blue will live on after we're gone.

Shitfish and Mastertone

Maypo

Most Friendships are formed by caprice or chance,
mere confederacies in vice or leagues in folly.

QUESTION OF BALANCE

A BLACK CHEVELLE PEELED out of a side road and cut us off, fishtailing back and forth across the double yellow line, smoke billowing from its hind quarter as it burned 150 feet of rubber and shot into the distance at 3 times the speed limit.

"Look at that damn fool," my mom said. "He's gonna kill someone driving like that."

I wanted the driver's autograph. It was the greatest display of muscle-car might I had ever seen. We entered the cloud of smoke and the squeal of tires and roar of engine echoed in my mind, drowning out my mom's rant about reckless driving.

We pulled into our driveway and the transgressing Chevelle was parked in front of our house with my brothers checking it out from every angle: 1970 Chevy SS 454, dual racing stripe, cowl injection, hood locks, LS6 upgrade. Leaning against the grill was Norm, my oldest brother's best friend, back from Nam. A swag of blond hair crossed his forehead, and he lit a cig, proud as could be of his overpowered jet.

Our mom dressed him down worse than a drill sergeant, railing on about his lack of self-control, responsibility and judgement.

Mark Cavanagh | 1

Norm scuffed at the pavement, hating to let our mom down. When she finally let up, he said, "Sorry, I'm just excited to be back."

Norm garnered four speeding tickets in the next six months for violations over 100 miles per hour. His final offense takes place in a school zone where he was clocked at 110. The arresting officer testified that he had never seen a more wanton disregard for the law. The judge revoked Norm's license, and he was at a crossroad. He knew he'd get in serious trouble if he hung around Swansicut, so Norm signed up for a second tour of duty.

"There's only one place in the world where I can drive," he said, "and that's Nam."

Buck and Lyle trespassing

While Norm was off fighting the war, the Sullivan brothers got on with their lives. Sausage married his high-school sweetheart, Crash, and joined the Army Reserves. Cosmos completed an engineering degree at Boston University and started a med-tech company in California. Buck went to Providence College and took a Philosophy course taught by our brother-in-law, Whippo, thinking it was a gut. Buck nearly flunked. I finished high school with average grades but got into Brown to play hockey. Our cousin Lyle played so much b-ball on the inner-city tarmac that he grew an afro and went to Boston College for hoops. In our spare time, we hopped the fence of the Swansicut Water Supply and fished the forbidden waters.

National Archives

Norm

In the Spring of 1972, with 36 days left on his second tour of duty, Norm was ordered to cross a rice paddy by a green-horn graduate of West Point. Norm saw movement in the trees on the far side of the bog and felt danger in his gut. He had seen settings such as this turn into killing fields and he wanted no part of it, but he could not refuse a direct order. With members of the 11th Calvary Regiment, Norm set out to cross the paddy.

Members of the 11th Calvary Regiment

They walked in single file, carrying weapons that had seen them through countless recon missions. Norm toted his machine gun and walked behind the point man who scanned for mines. Norm thought about killing his Lieutenant and leaving him face down in the shallow water, but he didn't need a murder charge.

The lead man stepped on a mine and all hell broke loose. Shrapnel tore through Norm, shredding him apart. Machine guns erupted on the far side of the bog, pinning the squad in a firestorm. Norm would have died there had his buddies not dragged him out. Multiple transfusions in a chopper, five unconscious days in a field hospital, and a long trip back to the U.S. left Norm in the Chelsea Navy hospital with a bleak prognosis: shattered legs and arms, damaged internal organs, deep lacerations from the neck down.

Sausage went to see him and brought back the bad news: the wounds to Norm's legs would never heal. Someday, he'd lose them at the knee. The far-away war came home with Norm and the images on the TV were never the same.

When Norm was cleared for a daytrip from the hospital, Sausage eased him into our father's station wagon and brought him home for a Sunday meal. Norm stood in the kitchen wearing a full body cast, propped up on crutches, right arm in a sling, feet in orthotic boots. The last time I saw him, he was 6'2" and 210 pounds of strapping buckshot. Now he was 5'10, shaped like a broken barrel and smelling of blood. But there was that smile of his, that impish grin, that told me Norm had not changed.

"Maypo," he said, "how's it hanging?"

He pulled me to him with his good arm, the one bandaged from the elbow down, and it was like getting hugged by a mummy. I was ready to cry for what the war had taken away, but I didn't comprehend Norm's survival instinct. He would kick the crap out of these injuries and fight battles for countless disabled vets.

"Let's go for a ride around the Res," Norm said. "I want to see the water and take in the air. It'll all come back."

I didn't know if he was talking about his body or soul.

I helped Norm into our wide-tracking Catalina and took him for a tour around the reservoir. We parked on the causeway that splits the Res in two and dark water ran away on both sides of the road. Norm rolled down his window and drew in the air with glassy contentment. Norm was home.

I crushed a lump of red Lebanese hash into a homemade pipe and torched it with a lighter. I had never smoked with Norm, but I wanted to show him I had grown up in his absence.

Norm toked deeply and coughed hard, resetting a couple of ribs. He winced in pain but smiled all the same. He said they smoked so much weed in Nam that they didn't get high, they were high.

I felt him slipping back there and pushed an eight-track into the stereo. Jim Morrison sang "Break on Through to the Other Side" and Norm was seized by an idea. He had to buy a record, immediately.

I guided the blue Catalina to a strip mall in Johnston and Norm had me dig his wallet out of his breast pocket. I asked him what record he wanted me to buy, but he said he was going in.

Norm released the passenger door with the hook of his left hand and fell to the pavement. I ran around to pick him up and he was laughing. I propped him against the hood and reached into the back seat for his crutches. I turned around and Norm was lurching across the parking like something out of Night of the Living Dead. He spooked an old lady coming out of a store and disappeared into the record shop. Moments later he returned with an LP tucked into his sling.

"The Moody Blues," he said. "A Question of Balance. Is that fucking perfect or what?"

The album cover was awash in psychedelic whirls. A hand reached out from ominous clouds, questing, searching.

"You like the Moody Blues?" Norm asked.

I'd never heard of the Moody Blues, but I didn't admit it.

"No, I'm more into Hendrix."

"Maypo, you've got shit for brains. Hendrix is noise. This is music."

He shook the album in my face like creed. Then he laughed a forgiving chuckle.

"I love you, Maypo," he said. "You're a fucking piece of work."

Norm returned to the hospital and healed enough for discharge. He holed up at Sausage and Crash's apartment and the album went on the turntable where it played over and over. There was something in the men's voices that Norm needed to hear – a cry for unity, a call to higher ground. He chain-smoked, drank handles of rum, and picked off birds out the window with a .22 rifle. At night, he slept with the TV on so if he woke up screaming with bullets flying and bombs going off, he'd know where he was - there are no TVs on the battlefield. Norm was not in a good place. He had nowhere to go, no job, no prospects, and no idea what to do with his life. His body was a wreck, he was in constant pain, and he felt lost. Norm needed balance and on some level he found it in the Big Blue.

Norm, A.K.A. Bobby

Life is not the wick or the candle - it is the burning.

William Shakespeare

Origins Of the Blue

Norm takes over the lead here. When he writes, you get the feeling that he's smiling the whole time. He and Sausage founded the Society after a fateful night of fishing at the Swansicut Reservoir.

∽

THEY WERE A handful of human beings, youthful friends brought together by their common interests. They were power forwards, quarterbacks, pond hockey legends, and sniffers. Apart from the endless hours of competition in every athletic venue, and sleep of course, there was only enough time left in a day for two things: fishing and pooty pursuit.

Now, there are some within the tender gender who may find this last phrase objectionable. But let's not be too judgmental. Afterall, fishing and pooty pursuit fall within the same general category. The truth is that in this vast universe that we call home, there are only two things that smell like fish, and one of them is fish. It is therefore quite logical that a group of young, unattached and hormone-exploding teens would devote their young lives to these very pursuits. Our story is centered on one of these continuing escapades.

It all began in the early 1960's when two of our founding fathers discovered that the best fishing hole in the Northern Hemisphere was located a half mile down the road. This was fishing heaven, 102 miles of pristine shoreline on a clear, clean, freshwater lake with a sandy bottom. Naturally, there were some drawbacks. The land was posted. No fishing, no hunting, no trespassing. No fucking way.

We could never abide by such an outrageous set of laws. The way we saw it, God had carved out a Mecca of freshwater game fish that was unrivaled. Seven-pound largemouth bass, schools of smallmouth two to five pounds, pickerel that rivaled Northern Pike in both size and fight, and hornpout to die for when fried over a fire with flour and light seasoning. No man should be denied such joy. We were not. I give you this information because it is wholly relevant to the birth of "The Society."

In our younger days we were cautious, aware of the stiff penalties for invasion of the Swansicut Reservoir sanctuary. But boys being the sub-species that they are, we were also aware of the risk rewards. We traversed the woods and fire roads leading to our fishing Valhalla in a manner that would make an Army Ranger proud. We made good use of the abundant camouflage, wore dark colors and fished at dusk whenever possible. Naturally, there were some daylight incursions, but these were almost always complicated by narrow escapes from local law enforcement or state fish and game officials.

I guess you could say we were fortunate. We had been fishing our favorite haunt for several years without getting caught, a place we called "the point." But I will never forget May 30th, 1972, Sausage and Crash's first wedding anniversary. Sausage had a grand evening planned. A dozen roses, a candlelit dinner, and a lengthy frolic in the holy mackerel. But first, he and I had to make a short visit to the point. I had just finished my second tour in the Nam or, more precisely, it had just finished me. I had been back on my feet for maybe a month and this was to be my first hook-up since returning to the world.

We got an early start, too early perhaps, but then there were other plans. The seriousness of my wounds required that we drive the half mile that we would have otherwise walked and Sausage dropped me off at the historical cemetery that guarded the entrance to the point. Then he parked the car about two hundred yards up the road just around a sharp curve. The short walk through the woods took about 15 minutes. I shuffled along in my blood-stained plaster of Paris leg irons wearing giant space shoes over my casts which allowed me to walk fairly well on level ground. Finally, we arrived at the point, the late afternoon sun bouncing off the glassy lake. The water was calm and the fish were getting ready to have a fist fight to see which one would graze my line first. Within minutes I had a tremendous strike. I knew instantly this was a big one and yelped with excitement, "Come to Papa, you nasty bastard."

Sausage gave pause to watch the spectacle of me trying to reel in the big one with two broken legs and a broken arm. It was like watching a one-legged show dog at the NY Kennel Club. I was about a minute into the fight when my line became snarled in a typical FUBAR (fucked up beyond all repair). I was clearly frustrated and the three Percodans I took 30 minutes before were only adding to my show dog appearance. I was reduced to barking expletives when Sausage snatched my snarled web of monofilament and proceeded to untangle the mess.

Anxious to see what kind of monster was hooked at the other end, I watched in a drug-reduced stupor, oblivious to pain but acutely aware of my surroundings. I didn't have much to work with at this point, but I had been blessed with incredible audio accuracy and was aware of something in the woods to our rear. I alerted Sausage who dismissed it as one of my many hallucinations.

"I'm telling you, I think someone is coming."

Sausage replied, "Assuming it's him, it's not like we're going to run away now are we?"

Sausage handed me the pole and I began to reel. Much to my surprise, the fish had come closer to the bank. As I took up the slack, he swirled giving us our first glimpse of his large frame.

"It's a beauty," Sausage quipped with excitement.

As the fish broke the surface, we gasped in amazement. This was the biggest pickerel either of us had ever seen. He was at least four pounds, huge for the species. At this moment, a voice to our rear said, "Hold it right there, you're under arrest."

We turned to see Mattison, an employee of the Swansicut Water Authority and living proof that at some point in time Howdy Doody had slipped his woody to a bantam rooster. This guy was 5 foot nothing with a slender build. He had a pronounced overbite and a commanding demeanor like that of Don Knotts. Now if you put all of those intimidating features together with a badge and a can of mace, it's easy to understand why the Sausage and I were quaking in our shoes and space shoes, respectively.

"Surrender those fishing poles and come with me," he said.

I looked at Sausage and he at me. We shrugged our shoulders.

"Bite my flubadub," Sausage replied.

I looked in amazement and thought… a confrontation. This is

gonna be great. I whispered to Sausage, "Let's pants the weasel and throw his ass in the lake."

"A lot of help you'll be," Sausage replied.

So we began our walk back to the blacktop. Sausage took the point and I followed along at a brisk half mile per hour. Mattison began poking me in the back in an effort to get me to hurry. I told him, "I've spent the last two years killing people I didn't know. It would certainly be different to kill some mother fucker I didn't like."

I could probably have gotten away with it. I carried a letter from my shrink that clearly stated my elevator didn't go all the way to the top floor. Sausage turned around in amazement and thought… a confrontation, oh shit! I had a serious reputation for violence and, at the sight of my rage, Mattison skedaddled his skinny ass down the path back to his Swansicut Water Supply jeep. Now this was an interesting situation. Howdy Doody was radioing for help and we were unsupervised in the woods. Sausage, to whom I give credit, was a U.S. Army drill instructor and his evade and escape mentality kicked into high gear.

"Come on Norm, we're going cross-country," he stated in his commanding voice.

"The fuck you say," was my thoughtful reply.

This had all the makings of a real horror show. I flashed back to the night that Sausage and Crash had driven to Boston and picked me up at the Chelsea Naval Hospital. They were taking me home for the weekend. There were a couple of small problems however. I was in a body cast and confined to a wheelchair. There was a Nor'easter blowing and a good foot of snow already on the ground. Not a problem however for the three stooges. Crash bundled my legs in quilts and busted my balls the whole time. Sausage took control and wheeled me out the door and down the wheelchair ramp from Ward 114. His car was parked around the corner and down the hill, a good 35-degree angle. We had some pretty good momentum when we turned the corner and came face to face with an oncoming snowplow. There was only one thing to do. We bailed into a snowbank created from earlier passes of the plow. My scream could be heard on Bunker Hill, I'm sure.

"You're a pussy, Norm," Sausage said. He knew how to goad me. "It's my anniversary and I need to get home, so let's do it."

What Sausage was proposing was a 400-yard journey through the woods of New England. It was spring and there was good cover, so we went for it. We hooked a right and headed off in the direction of home. I held myself up and moved from one tree to the next. There was certainly no shortage of trees. For that matter, there was no shortage of downed limbs, rocks, ledge, and the ever-present fieldstone walls. I was right; it was a fucking horror show. I guess 15 minutes had passed when the first patrol car arrived on the scene. Its spotlight scanned the woods to our left with a voice yelling into the darkening sky, "We know you're in there, come out with your hands up."

The patrol car inched along trying to catch us in his ray of light.

"Do you think this guy has been watching too much TV?" Sausage joked.

"Absofuckingtively," I answered.

We had reached the point where the entire scenario was funny. Red, a little freckled-faced moron, had now joined in the search. He cruised the blacktop in his 4WD shouting into the night. We laid low for 20 minutes or so and, when we were sure that the search had been discontinued, we made our way out to the road. Sausage walked me back to the big house where his parents lived. I called for a ride home and began to lick my wounds. I had broken both leg casts and was bleeding at a pretty good pace, but my problems were nothing compared to those of the Sausage. He was already late for his first anniversary, and he still had to retrieve his car.

Sausage threw on some jogging shorts, a sweatshirt, ball cap and sneakers. He took off down the road disguised as the roadrunner.

As he approached the final curve he ran literally into the Swansicut Police, a wrecker, and Howdy Doody himself.

"That's him, that's one of them," Howdy yelled in his little soprano voice.

The story goes that the Sausage was cuffed, taken to the station, fingerprinted, mug shot, booked for trespassing, and thrown in the slammer. I think he was cavity searched but he steadfastly denies this. Sausage made bail around midnight and was rather tight-lipped about his punishment from the Crash. I've since learned that his dinner was out of a cereal box and he didn't get to frolic in the holy mackerel. That seemed appropriate. Afterall, he was a fucking criminal.

Sausage called the next morning and informed me of his plight. He could get a deal if I would go to the police and turn myself in. I agreed with some hesitation. He picked me up and we drove to the police station. Upon our arrival, we were sent directly to the Chief's office. The look on his face was priceless.

"What the fuck happened to you?" he asked, scanning me from head to space shoes.

"Stepped on a land mine," I said.

"Geezus son, I had no idea."

"Well, that's just how it goes, sir. Wrong place, wrong time."

"Look guys, I don't want to be a hard ass about this but I've got a report here that you threatened the life of Officer Mattison. Which one of you did that?"

"Oh, that was definitely me, sir," I replied. "But I should tell you that he pushed me."

"What the hell were you doing fishing in the reservoir? You both should know better."

The barrister that is hidden within the Sausage was compelled to speak. "Chief, I'll tell you my best friend here made only one request of me when he returned from Nam. He asked me to take him to catch a fish. I thought about it for a while and it seemed the most normal request he ever made. The operative phrase in the whole equation was ***catch a fish.*** I only know one place where that is positively assured."

The Chief nodded his head, and "the reservoir" rolled off his tongue as if it were a rehearsed line. I was amazed by his keen sense for the urgency that we felt. I had to ask, "Tell me the truth, Chief. Have you ever cast a line on those troubled waters?"

He didn't have to answer. The Chief took down the vital info relative to my surrender. Name, address, phone, and DOB. He gave us the five-minute pitch and summed it all up by stating that if we were ever caught on reservoir property again, we would go to jail. We were summarily discharged after giving our word that we would never be caught again.

Sausage and I piled into his maroon Valiant and took the backroads home. It was a ride that would forever more change the direction of our Society. As we drove past the most beautiful sights the reservoir had to offer, we each realized that a chapter of our lives was over. It was sad and neither of us had much to say. But that moment of silence was just that, a moment. I lit a joint and passed it to Sausage.

"Do you know what this means?" I asked.

"Yeah, it means we can't fish the reservoir anymore. Shit, that really sucks."

Sausage was bummed.

"Not exactly," I replied.

"What do you mean?"

"I mean we're gonna have to take this show on the road."

"Fishing trips?" Sausage asked, a smile spreading from ear to ear."

"Exactly," I said.

Bobby

If you ain't fishing, you're fritterin' away your existence.

CHARLIE COOK

THE FIRST RENDEZVOUS

We all have appointments to keep with ourselves, things we must do to be happy and whole. Fishing is one of those things for the Big Blue. After getting banned from the Res, Sausage leaped into action in the Spring of 1973. **Norm recounts the first fishing trip** and the event that earned him his Society nickname, "Bobby."

I T ALL BEGAN on the shores of Big Lake in Princeton, Maine and, while it lacked the mayhem that we became known for in later years, it certainly had its moments. Sausage organized our escape to the northland and our cast of characters was small. There was Sausage, his brother Buck, myself, and an obscure Saturday Night Fever type whom we called Testiclese. The plan called for a 4 AM departure from Glendale, Rhode Island, where Sausage and Crash lived in a third-floor tenement apartment. If we left early enough, we could avoid the Boston traffic and be well on our way by the time most normal people awakened.

Sausage and I were elected to drive. He trusted his slant six Plymouth Valiant and I was the proud owner of a new Ford Pinto hatchback. Now, for those of you who can't remember this sporty version of the Radio Flyer Wagon, let me refresh you. The rear seats folded down and yielded enough room for two fishing poles and four paper bags of groceries. It had four speeds forward and one in reverse. Mine was a gold shade of brown and looked like a big turd. On the positive side, the elastic bands that provided its power were still under warranty and I was sure that it would survive the trip.

I left the driveway at 3:30 am with a sandy crust around my eyeballs. I was balancing a cup of Maxwell House in my lap, sucking on a Marlboro, and trying my best to negotiate the narrow country roads that I so fondly called home. I'd driven less than a half a mile when I hit a pothole the size of Crater Lake. The hot coffee burned my nuts and I dropped my cigarette, setting the deluxe brown carpet to smoldering. I could only hope that the journey would improve.

I pulled into the Sausage's driveway and was greeted by my fellow Blues. We loaded up the several cases of beer that Testiclese had appropriated from his job as a state liquor inspector and pointed our chariots north. We drove through Boston an hour later, past the twenty or so miles of Atlantic coastline that is New Hampshire and made Portland, Maine in under two hours and fifteen minutes. It was 6:30 AM and I was wearing my coffee, swilling my second beer, and struggling to keep pace with the Valiant at twelve o'clock. We made good time until we hit Bangor and, at that point, the trip took on a different look.

We steered north out of Bangor on a road that was used almost exclusively by the Great Northern Paper Company. Giant trucks hauling trees to market sped by, seemingly forcing us off the road at every turn. There were ninety miles of this road ahead and my knuckles were already white from the death grip that I had on the steering wheel. I've never been more terrified and yet a prevailing spirit of adventure pushed us forward. Every so often, we passed a scenic vista giving way to pink granite mountains that encircled some unknown but spectacular lake. There wasn't any question that the Sausage was leading us to a sportsman's paradise.

When we finally pulled into Princeton, the sun was directly overhead. Princeton was a small town and every bit as charming as the mythical Brigadoon. Sausage wheeled into a bait and tackle shop on the shores of Big Lake. I guided the brown turd in beside him and we sat, staring at each other in disbelief.

"Do you believe that fucking road?" I asked.

Sausage just rolled his eyes. Buck was still a little green around the gills and it was obvious that the drive up had been harrowing from the passenger's seat. We breathed a collective sigh of relief and entered the lakeside shop. This place was like a L.L. Bean franchise. They sold every kind of gizmo you could think of, from kayaks to toboggans. Sausage looked like he was taking inventory, slowly moving down each isle and eyeballing every gadget in the place. We only needed three things, a fishing license, worms, and directions to the local Indian reservation. I dragged Sausage out and we drove to the Indian campground where we were greeted by Chief Ain't Got No Teeth.

"How," Sausage quipped.

It was apparent that the Chief had heard that line at least once before and did not share in the humor, but he gave us a good site, right on the shore, with a sandy beach, and not too far from the water closet. Our first order of business was to set up the camp. Sausage had put his good name on the line and borrowed everything we needed from a co-worker Dick Diggle. We had a family size tent, cots, cooking utensils, Coleman lanterns, and rain tarps. We had given our word that we would care for these things as if they were our own. Dick was a terrific guy but obviously not a very good judge of character.

The tent was a huge canvas job. You know the type, it looks like army surplus and smells like army surplus. Well, setting it up was a real pain in the ass. I do recall, however, that there was a tall center pole and that the pole vault was destined to be a scheduled competition.

When we made the camp all that it could be under the influence of six or seven beers, we set out in different directions to work the shoreline. We employed all of our fishing skills and used a wide variety of baits including spinners, rubber worms, real worms, surface lures, and anything else that came to mind. I should tell you right here that the fishing sucked, at least for us. We had no boat and certainly couldn't rent one since we had spent most of our money on provisions like chips and nuts and cookies and important shit like that. So, with the coffers nearly empty, the fishing bordering on pathetic, and an overall sense of gloom setting in, we steered a new course in the direction of getting completely wasted.

It was the responsibility of each to take his turn in preparing meals. Testiclese was first out of the blocks and offered up a hearty bowl of Dinty Moore. He garnished the offering with a side of oyster crackers, a loaf of French bread, and a bottle of Yukon Jack. We were all in agreement. This guy could cook! The Jack circled the campfire and with each pass, our speech and cognitive powers diminished. We passed the time by critiquing our day and dazzling each other with memories of high school conquests. A heavy fog rolled in over the lake and the conversation wound down as we each began to enjoy the nocturnal grandeur of Big Lake. Suddenly, Sausage jumped to his feet.

"Fuck this," he said. "I want to catch fish. Someone come up with an idea" he scowled.

Buck, who rarely said anything, obviously had Huck Finn as a summer reading assignment. "Let's build a raft," he said with a look of excitement in his eye.

"Go fuck yourself" I replied.

It wasn't a bad idea, but it clearly fell within the purview of work and that was out of the question. Testiclese was all for nude wade fishing. That idea seemed to catch the Sausage's fancy for just a minute as an excuse to take off his clothes. I had zero input and was now taking double hits on the whiskey. Sausage's frustration was apparent when he proclaimed to one and all that he would resolve this little problem in the morning. I just loved it when he acted presidential. We retired to the sanctuary of our giant tent and slowly slipped into the kind of sojourn that produces snoring, grunting, farting and piss hard-ons.

Sausage was up at the crack of dawn, a man on a mission. The plan was to drive into town and gather enough intelligence on local fishing to improve our plight. The operative word here was intelligence and armed only with pulsating hangovers, I didn't give the plan much chance for success. We pulled into a lakeside restaurant and ordered four cups of mud, further depleting our cash reserves. Sausage learned of a river that separated Maine from Canada, the Saint Croix. It was only a few miles away and, while nobody seemed to know much about the fishing prospects, it was, in fact, our only viable alternative.

We drove north out of Princeton on the narrowest of dirt roads. Every few hundred yards or so, the road would fork and we would cross some sort of makeshift log bridge. We inched along weaving our way between giant potholes and collectively wondering if we were going the right way. All of a sudden, a raging river appeared directly ahead.

"This must be the place," Sausage said.

We each nodded our approval. It certainly was an interesting spot. There was a massive cement superstructure that spanned the river and supported some sort of pipeline. The river was very swift and deep, at least fifteen feet at the banks. We would fish with four different baits until someone got lucky and that happened immediately. Buck tied into something that fought like a Small Mouth Bass and the pace of the river added a new element to our excitement.

"What are you using?" Testiclese asked.

"A rubber worm with some split shot," Buck answered.

There was the typical mad dash for the tackle boxes as everyone wanted to get in on the action. Buck continued to fight the fish as we all got giddy with anticipation. When the fish finally broke the surface, we were all quite astonished. This was without question the ugliest fish that any of us had ever seen. We had no idea what the fuck it was, but it put up a hell of a fight and we were finally having fun.

"Now this is what we came here for, boy," Sausage enthused.

At this moment, a small forest came floating downstream. I'd seen this shit in the movies but this was the real McCoy, log jams on their way to market. The logs floated by every twenty minutes and to this day, it ranks, at least for me, as one of life's great spectacles.

We caught a shit load of fish, had them on stringers and, by golly, as soon as we figured out what we had then we'd have something. It was mid-afternoon when we started back to the reservation. We were inching our way along the dirt road and mind fucking each other with assorted put downs and stinging insults when we came face to face with an oncoming pick-up truck. There were two guys inside, obviously locals. Now we couldn't have known that this was Jethro and his second cousin/brother-in-law Chet. Sausage pulled as far to the right as he could and with his arm extended waved the truck to stop.

"What the hell are you doing?" Buck asked with some trepidation.

"I'm going to find out what kind of fish these are," Sausage replied.

The two vehicles pulled up, side by side. Sausage explained our dilemma to the driver and he agreed to take a look at our catch of the day. The driver's expert opinion was immediately called into question because he was uglier than the fish in question. We all exited and made our way to the rear of the car. Jethro leered into the trunk and grunted in true swamp Yankee fashion.

"'Em are pickerel," he said.

We chuckled in unison and asserted that we knew what pickerel were and these were not pickerel. Jethro seemed genuinely hurt. He lifted the stringer to get a better look.

"Well then, I reckon 'em are LY," he said, quite seriously.

We all struggled to hold back our laughter when Jethro's kin chimed in, "Yeah, dem's all bucks."

Sausage slammed the trunk lid and thanked the two gentlemen for their time. Testiclese said for all to hear, "I've seen this movie."

"Yeah, me too," I said.

We were laughing so hard at this point that I damn near pissed on myself. Sausage hit the gas and kicked up a bit of Maine real estate in the process. In an absolute howl, we moved on down the road. As the laughter started to fade, Buck asked, "What the fuck is an LY?"

We laughed some more. A few minutes had passed when Sausage noticed the pick-up truck in the rear-view mirror. He moved up behind us rather quickly and camped on our rear bumper. Sausage sped up, so did the truck. Buck was looking a bit worried and asked, "What do you think they want?"

"Where is Ned Beatty when you need him?" Sausage inquired.

Testiclese answered, "You mean, Bobby."

"Who's Bobby?" Buck asked.

Sausage reminded Buck of the little fat guy in the movie, "Deliverance," who crawled around in his underwear, made sounds like a pig, and got stuffed by the hillbilly.

"Oh, that Bobby," Buck acknowledged.

"I've been giving this some thought," Sausage explained. "If we're forced to make a run for it, there is only one of us who can't run and has no chance of getting away. All eyes shifted to me. "I guess that makes you Bobby."

Once again, I was victimized by my own battle scars. Well, rest assured I wasn't going down without a fight. "Stop the car," I yelled.

Sausage skidded to a halt. I jumped out and reached under the front seat as if to retrieve a weapon. As I stood, I made a motion to chamber a round in a semi-automatic handgun. With my right hand concealed from view, I motioned for the would-be rapist to get out of the truck. The fish-eyed fool and his goat-stroking sidekick backed up and beat a hasty retreat. It was a good bluff and we had been successful, but the damage was done. I knew it about a mile down the road when Sausage looked at me and said, "Good job, Bobby."

Back at camp, we had some lunch, drank some beers and got the pole vault competition underway. It was at this point that we discovered the perfectly round hole in the floor of our borrowed family tent. There was no way for us to know that the lantern would get so hot. Sausage was visibly shaken.

"Dick is going to be pissed."

"Sausage," I consoled, "Dick will certainly understand that this was an accident."

There were no words for the remorse that we felt. Buck is one of the more decent humans on the planet and always in tune with the feelings of others. However, on this particular trip, his first real getaway with the older guys, he was mostly drunk and refreshingly insensitive. Buck surveyed the gaping hole, staggered backward and said, "Look at the bright side. When Dick sees the big hole it may divert his attention away from the dozens of cigarette burn holes."

Buck was right, there were small holes scattered all about the tent. In the right light, they resembled some of the more recognizable constellations. Sausage was in shock.

"Damn, I didn't even see those."

"Well that just proves my point," Buck said. "Dick probably won't see them either."

Sausage shook his head and said, "I'm getting drunk."

Testiclese nodded his approval. "Now there is a novel idea."

That evening, Sausage and Testiclese tried their hands at some surface lures. Buck and I stayed behind to prepare the evening meal. We wrapped a five-pound ham in 25 feet of aluminum foil, seasoned it with a can of fruit cocktail and threw the whole mess directly into the hot coals. I took the cap off a bottle of White Label Scotch

Whiskey, threw it away, lit a joint, and took up a culinary vantage point. Buck lit out for the outhouse with a roll of toilet paper. I wished him Godspeed and visually followed his staggering, drunk ass from my fireside perch. He hadn't even reached the road when a full-figured red head fell in behind our young Buck.

Big Red, as she became affectionately known, was staying at the adjacent campsite. The setting sun silhouetted the cheeks of her rounded posterior which were protruding from the confines of her bright yellow shorts. I thought it a bit odd that she would pick this exact moment to visit our spider infested community water closet, but when you've got to go, well....

Our fellow anglers returned before Buck and, when they inquired as to his whereabouts, I brought them up to speed. We passed the scotch around and awaited Buck's return. Mind you, there really wasn't anything unusual about this whole scenario, but it did provide an opportunity to divert attention away from myself and my newly acquired nickname. Within minutes, Buck returned and was fair game for my barrage of stingers. I was prepared to pull out all of the stops. I was goal directed and determined to shift everyone's attention elsewhere. Big Red was like a gift from above. She was my only salvation at this point or so I thought. Sausage saw right through my little plot and he was having none of it.

"Bob," he said, "you're a good man and we love you, but nothing short of total mass amnesia is going to change the fact that you are the BOBMAN."

There was no doubt about it. I needed a miracle. We put a serious dent in the five pounds of ham, which came out rather well and the side of beans and scotch earned everyone's applause. Our barbaric ancestors would have been proud. After dinner, we all kicked back with a cheap cigar and watched another heavy fog roll in across the lake. The fire was stoked, our bellies were full, we were seriously fucked up, and the world was a pretty cool place. The bull shit flowed at its customary pace when the night was interrupted by a cry for help.

Some guy was caught out on the lake in the pea soup fog. He'd seen the glow of our fire and slowly approached the beach. We welcomed him to the best of our ability. I mean, we were in no shape for visitors. Nevertheless, it was not now nor would it ever be our habit to turn away a fellow angler or a man in need. His name was Bill and he worked in a shoe factory down in the Manchester, N.H. area.

"God, something smells good," Bill said, his eyes widening.

"Are you hungry?" we asked.

"I could eat the south bound end of a north bound skunk," he replied.

Sausage set him up with a hearty plate of ham and beans. He sucked down a few cold ones, shared our scotch, and even took a few hits from the joints that were circling the fire. Bill was having a great time and more than once had remarked about his good fortune.

"You guys are terrific," he said.

"Bill," Testiclese interrupted, "you're welcome to spend the night but you'll have to sleep with Bobby."

I would have gladly choked the life out of Testiclese at this point, but I had an aversion to standing. Once again, I was the target. The laughter subsided and we heard the faint cry of what sounded like a search party out on the lake. The slow hum of an outboard motor moved ever closer and the searching voices became clearer.

"Bill, you're last name isn't 'Dick Head' by any chance, is it?" I asked.

"Yeah, that would be my friends. They come out looking for me every night at about this time."

"You do this every night?" Testiclese questioned.

"Yeah, but you got to understand, these guys are the worst cooks I've ever known and they ran out of beer two days ago."

The flim flam man, Bill Dick Head, had duped us. It was a classic maneuver, and we all agreed that Bill would have made one hell of a Blue. We said our good-byes and sent Bill off packing with his buddies, the chug of their motor fading into the night fog. We laughed at Bill's antics for awhile and turned in for the night. We hadn't yet fallen asleep, arguing over who was going to get up and turn off the lantern, when we heard the sputter of an airplane engine.

"Damn, that's low," Testiclese said.

"It sounds like someone's in trouble," Buck added.

"It's probably another dick head trying to take advantage of our hospitality," Sausage chipped in.

We all exited the tent just in time to hear a single engine plane crash into the lake. We looked dumbfounded at each other. Someone was in need of help, but we had no boat and were too fucked up to help anyone at this point. There was an all-night rescue mission on the lake although we actually never saw anything. The fog was just too thick.

We broke camp in the morning and carefully stowed all of Dick's camping equipment in the rear of Sausage's car. He stared in disbelief at the ruined tent, his good name tarnished for all time. We loaded up four bags of trash and headed for the Indian dump where a dozen black bear were lined up as if standing at a buffet table. We discarded our trash and began the arduous trip home.

I called Norm in Texas and caught him napping on his back porch. He had moved south a few years ago because winters in the Northeast were hell on his body. He was fifty now and sporting a 7 handicap in golf. When I laid out the idea of gathering Big Blue stories in the form of a book, he was all for it so long as it didn't feel like work. He was, after all, retired. But something happened at the end of the Princeton trip that set a guidepost for the Society and Norm had left it out.

"Hey, I swore an oath thirty years ago. I'm not about to break it now."

"Decisions were made, Bob, actions were taken."

"We were married men, Maypo."

"I know that, but it's important to the history of the Big Blue."

Bob took a deep drag on something combustible and exhaled slowly. I could tell he was thinking it through. As a young man, Bob said and did whatever he wanted. But maturity had changed him. He was concerned with his legacy now, the story of his life as others would read it. Plenty of skeletons were out of the closet and he didn't want to drag any more.

"Bob," I said, breaking the silence.

"What?" he asked, as if I might have forgotten what we were talking about.

"I'm waiting."

He took another long drag, and I sensed he was blowing one smoke ring through the hole of another, an avoidance technique. Silence crackled on the line and finally Bob said, "I'll see what I can do."

A week later, this e-mail was in my box.

We left Princeton, all nursing serious hangovers, the worst of which belonged to Buck. We stopped at least ten times on the logging road for Buck to hurl. When we finally reached Bangor, it was painfully obvious that we could go no further. Buck was gray and ready to pass out. We checked into a hotel using our emergency plastic and Buck crawled into bed. As night descended on our tired butts, hunger set in and a road trip was inevitable. Sausage sent Testiclese and me to pick up sandwiches and a bottle of Pepto Bismal. We set out to find a restaurant that accepted plastic, our intentions wholly honorable.

The following incident has been sealed in the Big Blue archives for over thirty years, but at the insistence of my brothers, I tell it to you now. You will recall my introduction of the Saturday Night Fever type in the person of Testiclese. Well, he earned this comparison that night with his version of, "The City Boy Visits the Country Fucks." We drove through the unfamiliar streets of Bangor and happened on a hopping little joint called, "Broken Promises." The parking lot was filled with pick-up trucks and there were no shortages of gun racks in their rear windows.

"Pull in here," Testiclese yelled.

I guided the brown turd in between a couple of trucks and we walked inside. This was the place! We bellied up to the bar, ordered a couple of rum and cokes, and asked for a menu. Less than a minute had passed when a cute little thing approached Testiclese and asked him to dance. He was gone. He vanished into the mass of maniacs and dazzled everybody with his version of the funky fisherman. I knew that we weren't getting out of here anytime soon, so I ordered a sandwich and another drink. I'd seen this scene unfold more than once. Testiclese had gotten a whiff of some duck-butter and it was anyone's guess where this would lead.

Testiclese had been gone for about thirty minutes when he showed up at the bar. "Let's go," he said.

"Go where?" I asked.

"Back to her place. She's going to make some sandwiches for the guys and I think I'm going to get laid."

"And what the fuck am I going to be doing during all of this?" I asked.

Testiclese had all the answers. "That's the beauty of it. She has a roommate."

Did she ever. Behind Testiclese was his little brunette who looked like she just stepped out of a Matt Helm movie. Standing right next to her was a bleach blonde with a big smile and an even bigger ass. This girl reminded me of the village bicycle. You know! Everyone has had a ride. I didn't want to rain on the parade, but I was not the slightest bit interested. Testiclese was reduced to begging and therein lies my sin. I agreed to accompany him in his pursuit of the holy mackerel.

When we arrived at the girl's house, Testiclese disappeared into the back bedroom. I was left to parry the advances of the Phyllis Diller wannabe who was now clad in a flimsy nightgown. Her persistence called for drastic measures and, with the help of my ham and bean concoction from the previous night, I was able to summon up a raunchy bowel explosion. I made no attempt to excuse myself. For all I knew, I might have given birth to a brown tipper. I only knew that it worked. She called me disgusting and retreated to the sanctuary of her room.

I waited patiently for Testiclese, feet up on the coffee table, and tuned in the local news. I drifted off to sleep and, when I awoke, the sun had already tipped its brow. I banged furiously on the bedroom door and screamed, "The bus is leaving!"

I waited for Testiclese in the car and watched his comical retreat down the front stairs, dressing in the process. Testiclese knew that we had fucked up.

"Those guys are going to be pissed!"

"Oh, do you really think so?" I asked in my most sarcastic voice. "I hope that was some good pooty."

We didn't say much as we searched for the hotel, not even knowing if Sausage and Buck would still be there. Our reception was predictable. Sausage was pissed beyond words. He had not slept, worrying about our inconsiderate asses. He called hospitals, the police, and had every right to be mad.

I was mad at myself for the lack of good judgment that I had become famous for and, it goes without saying, this little adventure had far-reaching consequences. Pooty pursuit was banned from the Big Blue Rendezvous and Testiclese was kicked out of the Society. As for me, I probably would have gotten the boot as well, but then no one else would have so graciously accepted the role of Bobby.

Sausage and Smallmouth

A true friend is someone who sees you as a good egg
even though they know you are slightly cracked.

BERNARD MELTZER

GILEAD

FISHING AND WISHING amount to the same thing in the Big Blue. New England winters are cold, the days are short, and a man dreams of remote lakes and fish leaping into his net. He greases his reel, restocks his tackle box, and dresses lures as sure bets. He puts his faith in the act of fishing, the wish in every cast, and knows that catching a fish goes a long way to making life complete. But catching a fish is not essential - the pursuit is everything. At least that's what we tell ourselves when we're getting skunked.

Getting skunked is not acceptable to our brother Sausage. He'd rather fish an overstocked barrel than stalk elusive prey and come up empty-handed. *Fish* is what Sausage fishes for, not relaxation, not good company, not beautiful scenery. He likes hauling in fish until his arms are sore and his boots are bloody. Words like "rabid" come to mind and "obsessed."

An early spring trip to the pastoral town of Gilead, Maine, which hugs the Androscoggin River, sounded promising to Sausage. The river teems with small and largemouth bass, northern pike, black crappie, rock bass, yellow perch and pickerel. Sausage was anxious to catch any and all of them. He rounded up me, Buck and Bobby for a 4-day expedition. **Sausage swings into the lead here** about what happened on that trip and how the Big Blue Society got its name.

∽

On a chilly evening in early May of 1974, Bobby emerged from a New Hampshire state liquor store. He was accompanied by Maypo, who dutifully trudged along, burdened with four cases of beer. Bob made his way with a slight limp toward me and Buck, sitting in our car in the lot. Bob motioned for Maypo to set the cases on the hood of my car. He split the cardboard case, grabbed a six-pack and handed it through the window to Buck.

"Yo Maypo," he said, "Grab the rest of that shit and we're on our way."

"Whoa, Bob," Buck called, but it was too late. Nearly three cases of beer, along with Maypo and Bobby, disappeared into Maypo's truck. The "Bob" man was right. We were on our way. The Society was heading for Gilead, Maine.

Bob knew an old vet, from his travels with the DAV, who owned a classic, secluded farmhouse. Gilead was smack in the middle of prime New England trout waters. It didn't matter that we were several weeks early for the trout. After a long, snowy winter we felt the itch to simply go north and fish. None of us were adept at trout fishing. Nobody owned a fly rod. We had each other for company. We were fueled by a sense of adventure, some good booze, and a generous amount of Maypo's hash oil to season our smoker.

After two hours on the interstate, Maypo exited onto a narrow, two-lane blacktop. Maypo and Bob were a curious pair. For the most part, Maypo was a stable, motivated academic achiever at Brown University. He had dropped off the hockey team to devote more time to his studies. But, there was a wild thread that wove through Maypo and nobody tested the tensile strength of that thread more than Bob.

Maypo was drawn to Bobby's wild, uninhibited, high-wire perch. The difference was that Bobby lived there and Maypo just liked to visit. Whenever they got together, they fed off each other. Kindred spirits, birds of a feather, drawn to lunacy like moths to a porch light on a summer night.

After two hours of weaving through Maine back roads, we began to suspect that Maypo and Bob didn't know how to get to the Gilead farmhouse. Buck thought that they were lucky if they even knew where they were.

"I've counted at least twenty cans that they've thrown in the back of the truck," he said.

A short while later, Buck spotted a sign at an intersection that we had crossed an hour earlier. We sped up, passed the truck, and pulled over. Maypo pulled in behind. When Bob's bulk emerged, empty Bud cans cascaded out the door with him. Bob clutched a map.

"You see, Saus, we got this fuckin' map, but neither one of us can read it."

He had that grin on his face. It reminded me of a little kid who gets caught with his hand in the cookie jar. Bob's grin had a way of making you believe that he was simply walking by the cookie jar when the fuckin' cookies just kind of sucked his hand in. All the while, Maypo stared straight ahead. Whenever his feet moved, empty cans rattled.

Buck grabbed the map, located Gilead, and instructed Bobby that we were no more than five minutes away. "Oh," a contrite Bobby muttered.

Shortly after midnight, we roused the old vet who had fallen asleep at the kitchen table while waiting for us. He wearily showed us around and left us to settle in. A large kitchen, living room, oversized bath and two bedrooms downstairs. Two more bedrooms upstairs. We sat around, had a few beers, sampled Maypo's hash oil, and turned in.

Maypo, Buck and I grabbed a bedroom and left one downstairs

for Bob. There was something about Bob and beds, however, perhaps it was a legacy from Nam. The problem was he couldn't sleep in them. He chose the small couch in the living room and arranged himself in a fetal position. Within seconds, he was snoring like an old furnace.

The following morning we set out for town. We had a big breakfast and then split up to gather information on the hot fishing spots. An hour later, we met back at the car. Maypo was excited because he had been advised at the local tackle shop that although it was early in the season, yellow-tailed streamers were the lure of choice. In fact, he explained, just that morning a couple of guys who really seemed to know what they were doing had chosen those yellow-tail streamers.

"You mean these?" Buck said, presenting a fistful. Maypo was crestfallen.

"I guess we're the guys who looked like we knew what we were doing," I said.

"The only problem," Bob chuckled, is we never have a clue what we are fuckin' doin. We are the fuckin' Society man."

We spent the day exploring Gilead and other nearby towns. Whenever we spotted a body of water larger than a puddle, we threw a line in it. We stopped at streams and brooks. We hiked across meadows to beaver ponds. We had established the pot the night before. The biggest fish was worth money. The most fish caught merited a prize. If anybody caught a "shit" fish (other than a game fish) they would donate to the pot. Bobby had added a bet of his own. Whoever cut the largest fart earned ten dollars from everyone.

At the end of the day, we were tired and discouraged. The pot was safe. Nobody had even had a nibble. We consoled ourselves with thoughts of tomorrow. After all, it was only the first day of a four-day trip.

"I haven't heard a fart that has me worried yet either," Bob intoned on the way back to the farmhouse.

That night we cooked a ham and copious amounts of beans. We

baked potatoes and made a salad. Earlier, we had stopped in town to pick up more beer, some John Daniels for me and some scotch for Buck. Maypo splurged for a prime tequila.

The Blues had a certain reverence for the cocktail hour. It didn't matter that the first beer might wash down breakfast or that we had been dipping into the cooler all day. While dinner cooked we started the cocktail hour. The kitchen table became the bar and we tasted the various offerings. Conversation mellowed once we were freed from the pursuit of fish and had only ourselves, alcohol, and weed for companionship.

Bobby settled onto his couch, propped his feet on the coffee table and looked over at me.

"Sausage, boy, you remember Glendale a few years back before I went to Nam for the second time? You remember that summer? You were an innocent motherfucker, but I took care of all that. You remember Susan Tasca, Francine DeLeCroix, and the Durfee twins? You ever fuck any of them?"

I just looked at Bob because I know he didn't need an answer, but he did need an audience. He had Buck and Maypo's attention.

"Did you?" asked Buck, looking at Bob.

"Did I what?"

"Fuck 'em?" Buck shot back.

"Hell, yeah," Bob said, crushing out his Marlboro for emphasis.

"All of 'em?" Buck asked.

"Every fuckin' one of 'em," Bob assured him.

"Even the Durfee twins?"

"Yup, but not at the same time."

That evening in the farmhouse, while the ham baked in the oven, Bob took us on a verbal tour of his high school conquests. Buck listened and Maypo nodded knowingly. Brown University in the late 60s and early 70s was not a place for sexually reticent, emotionally conservative people. My brother Maypo had thrived.

As Bob spoke, I drifted back to the summer of 1967. I was lifeguarding, and Bob was stationed at a Nike missile site in Bristol. He was between tours in Nam and wild as the unruly hairs on Jimi Hendrix's head. He was over six feet tall, blond, blue-eyed, well-built, armed with that infectious grin and a prolific line of bull shit. The girls thought he was a young god and I think Bob would have agreed.

His parents worked the late shift and the house was empty at night. At least it was empty until we descended on it with guys and girls from all over town. Bob spent his time alternating between dives off the second story roof into the pool and trips to the bedroom with various willing partners.

At the end of that summer, Bob returned to Nam for a second tour of duty. He'd broken up with his favorite girlfriend and I think he was bored. Many returning vets simply missed the adrenaline of being in a war where the stakes were high and the ante was your life.

I had accompanied Bob to the train station with various friends and relatives. It was a somber scene. Just prior to boarding the train, Bob motioned me aside. I expected something emotional, sentimental. I felt my throat constrict and I promised myself I wouldn't cry.

"Saus, can you do me a big favor?"

"Sure," I said, avoiding his eyes. I would have jumped in front of the train for him at that moment.

"Do you know Ann Leonard?"

"Yeah," I said, "sure, she goes to Glendale High, doesn't she? Why?"

"Well, I kind of hooked up with her. She works as a carhop at the A & W and after work last night we went out. See, I kind of told her I would pick her up after school today."

"But Bob, you knew you were leaving today."

"I know," he said sheepishly.

"You didn't tell her?"

"No."

"Well, what do you want me to do?" I asked, mildly annoyed.

He glanced at his watch. "Right about now she is probably waiting for me outside the high school. Could you maybe swing by and kind of explain things?"

"Yeah," I mumbled, "after I leave here I'll swing by."

He shook my hand and enveloped me in a bear hug.

"Thanks, Buddy. I'm gonna miss you."

I held the tears and I turned away. I didn't want to look back.

"Hey, Sausage," he called softly. "There's something else you should know. I told her to wear a skirt but no underwear."

When we sat down to dinner, Bobby quickly shoveled a pint of beans into his mouth. He ladled a double serving onto his plate before touching his ham. "Fart food," he announced, winking at Buck.

Following dinner, nobody cleaned up. It was not the Blue way. Dishes were simply dumped in the sink. If someone needed a dish, they washed it. Maypo cleared a few cans and bottles from the kitchen table, produced a deck of cards, and shuffled like a Vegas dealer. Coins and dollar bills fueled the pot and blue smoke reeking of hash and Marlboro's settled over us. Buck lit a cigar and won three straight pots. As the clock ticked past midnight, the beans began to work and we serenaded each other with rectal eruptions. I felt a rumble in my abdomen and let a long, slow one escape. Maypo stopped dealing. Buck leaned over and inhaled deeply and the "Bob" man just smiled and shook his head slowly. The benchmark had been set. I'd almost destroyed a pair of Fruit of the Looms, but I was undoubtedly in first place.

Maypo was frustrated by poker and suggested we switch to Hi/ Lo Jack. He had just finished dealing when there was a knock on the door. We all shared the same thought - someone smelled the pot and called the cops. Maypo grabbed the bag and hurried into the bedroom. Buck dumped the ashtray in the trash under the sink and Bobby didn't move from the table. He reached for his Bud, leaned back in his chair, drained his beer in one swig and said, "Who is it?" in his most charming voice.

At first there was no response and then an unmistakable female voice said, "Can you help me, my boyfriend has had an accident!"

Buck opened the door and immediately stepped back. I've been surprised only a few times in my life. Once when I got a red Schwinn bike for my twelfth birthday and once when Francine DeLeCroix tried to extract my tonsils with her tongue in the back seat of my father's Buick Electra when I was sixteen years old.

Standing in the doorway was one of the most beautiful women I had ever seen. She was tall, slim, blonde-haired with blue eyes. Her lips were full and she had a faint half-smile. Peering into the kitchen of a secluded Maine farmhouse and beholding four unshaven faces with bulging, blood-shot eyes and gaping mouths did not seem to unsettle her.

Bob was the only one who could find words. He graciously invited her in. He cleared away some of the bottles littering the table and insisted she sit down. She explained that she and her boyfriend, along with another couple, were chaperoning a group of boys from her parish who were on a camping trip. Late that afternoon while hiking, her boyfriend had slipped and twisted his ankle. He was in a great deal of pain and they had set out to find a hospital. They had seen the lights on in our house and had stopped, hoping we might direct them to a hospital.

Bob introduced us and we learned that her name was Lynn. She accompanied us out to the car where we met Rick sitting in the front seat with his head arched back, grimacing in pain. We explained that we didn't know the area very well, but we imagined that the nearest hospital was not close by. He did agree, however, to come in and have a beer. Lynn also seemed to brighten at the prospect and Maypo and Buck made a makeshift chair with their hands and carried Rick into the house.

By now, it was well past midnight. Lynn and Rick settled in at our kitchen table and each sucked down two quick beers. Prior to their arrival, we were running low on energy and dangerously close to climbing into the sack. But now we were energized. Conversation flowed as freely as the beer and, as I popped open another round, I suggested to Maypo that he fetch something to make our guests truly comfortable. He disappeared into the bedroom and emerged a few minutes later. He approached the table with a wide grin and deposited a reefer the size of his little finger on the table in front of Bobby. Bob picked it up, held it to the light as if it was transparent. He sniffed it, inhaled deeply and said, chuckling, "Fuckin' Maypo." Buck shuffled his chair, sighed, and looked away. Perhaps he thought that with the simultaneous introduction of the weed and Bob's vulgarity, they would leave.

"Well, are you going to light that thing or hold it all night?" Lynn asked.

We all laughed. Bob lit the joint, passed it around and we peered at each other through the haze. Something was happening in that room. Rick seemingly was no longer in pain. Lynn continued to surprise us by lighting one of Bob's Marlboros. Buck poured everyone a shot of scotch and we toasted each other's company. Rick and Lynn, despite their misadventure and initial discomfort, had been enveloped by the aura and camaraderie of the Big Blue Society. Inhibitions melted away in the renewed wash of stimulants. Rick sat back, looked up at the crooked light fixture on the kitchen ceiling and informed us that he was, "Fuckin' wasted."

"Me too," said Lynn. "Hey, how's your ankle feelin'?"

"I don't know," Rick said, laughing, "cause I can't even fuckin' feel it anymore."

As the night slipped away and dawn approached, the party showed signs of breaking up. Lynn had confided, to our amazement, that she had recently left the convent.

"Thank God," Buck said. The thought of this beauty squeezed into the black and white of the Mercy habit, standing in front of salivating sixth graders had been too much for Buck.

"I thought of becoming a priest," Bob confessed.

Lynn seemed genuinely interested. "Did you study in a seminary?" she asked.

"Hell, no. I thought about it for all of ten seconds and just dismissed it," he said, snapping his fingers. "Hey, Sausage, can you imagine me as a priest? I mean me, a man of the cloth. Can you even remotely imagine the Bobman without even a little bit of pooty?"

"No way," I said.

Bob rose unsteadily from the table, took two tottering steps, tripped over the leg of his chair, and fell onto the table. Everything, including Bob, landed in a heap on the floor.

After the sound of the bottles and cans falling had faded, there were a few seconds without any sound. We were caught in the vacuum of deep laughter where at first, no sound comes out.

We eventually rose from our seats at the same time. Bob was still on the floor but he was laughing too hard to move. "Me a fuckin' priest," he managed to gasp between spasms.

As the rising sun glinted through the windows, Rick and Lynn left. Rick stood and pointed to his obviously broken ankle. He walked out without a limp. Lynn vanished forever like the smoke from a joint into the annals of the Big Blue Lore. In future years, on other Rendezvous, someone would invariably ask, "What do you think ever became of her?"

That morning we slept in. Around 11:00 I heard someone in the kitchen. I found Buck making scrambled eggs. The smell of coffee brought Maypo and Bob into the kitchen. They looked like two bears emerging from hibernation. We sat around the remnants of the kitchen table and surveyed the wreckage. Cans, bottles, butts, playing cards and scraps of food formed a kind of mosaic on the kitchen floor. We didn't have to talk. There was nothing to say. We all felt the same - severely hung over. The kitchen landscape focused our thoughts on the night before. A scene out of a Fellini movie. Bobby summed it up.

"Do you believe that shit from last night?" he asked nobody in particular.

At first nobody answered. Finally, Buck said, "That could only happen in the Society."

After breakfast, Bobby retreated to his couch and the rest of us cleaned up the kitchen. Deep inside there was a faint spark of order and cleanliness long ago instilled in us by our fastidious mother. Spirits gradually lifted as we worked to restore the kitchen. Beer farts smelling of rotten peat moss accompanied the swish of a broom and the clunk of dishes in the sink. Buck released a high, resonant moaner that reminded me of a coyote in heat. Bobby applauded from the next room and pronounced that Buck was now in first place. Maypo, in trying to keep up, confessed to a wet one. He went into the bedroom and emerged a few moments later, dangling his soiled underwear as if it oozed radiation and deposited it in the trash container under the sink.

We had no sooner begun to discuss the plan for our final afternoon when Bobby summoned us urgently to the living room. Bob was perched on his couch like an overstuffed bird on a nest. He wore only his Jockeys and he was surrounded by pillows. His belly hung over the lip of his shorts and his war scars glistened white on his torso. The gaping wounds on his legs stood in contrast to his absurd posture. He held his index finger in the air and, with one eye closed, his head was tilted towards the ceiling. He looked like a conductor poised in front of his orchestra, waiting for just the right moment to kick off an overture. And then it came. Low, basso profundo extending over at least five seconds. Then the booster kicked in, a sustained resonance that tapered to a staccato machine gun burst as Bob began to vibrate all over with his own laughter at the sheer magnitude of the thing. And finally, when there was a slight pause and we all thought it had to be over, there was a loud pop, followed by the sound of air hissing out of a balloon.

Bob popped his feet up on the coffee table, patted his stomach, scratched his scar and beamed at us. Buck, momentarily stunned, rushed over, snatched a cushion, sniffed it deeply, withdrew a ten from his pocket and tossed it in Bobby's lap. Maypo and I just looked at each other, reached for our wallets and paid homage to the Bobman.

"Hey, Buck, was there ever any doubt in who was gonna win this thing?" he asked.

"Bob, you are my hero," Buck said and sniffed the cushion again.

That afternoon we fished. We had returned to the local tackle shop in the hope of being turned on to a particular stream or body of water that might produce trout. We later found ourselves tossing our yellow tail streamers into a promising-looking pool at the base of a small waterfall. We had followed the clerk's instructions. After parking the car on a turnout, we had hiked more than a mile across open fields to arrive at the "pool." It was deep and dark and looked like a can't-miss spot. We fanned out around it and threw our yellow tail streamers in every nook and cranny. We fished for two hours without talking, concentrating only on fishing. We sensed defeat. Nobody caught even a single fish. Nobody had even a bite. Never had this happened to us.

On my last cast, however, I hooked what was determined to be the biggest fish of the trip. It also counted as the most fish caught. I swept the pool. My fish was smaller than my yellow tail streamer. I couldn't imagine why it had tried to eat something half again as big as itself, but it had. It was a garbage fish, a shit-fish, a fucking bluegill. The others denigrated my achievement, but nevertheless I accepted their money with the same aplomb as Bobby with the "fart" pot. I wanted someone to tell me I was their hero. Nobody said anything. In retrospect, it was a significant fish because we took from it our name, the Big Blue Society.

That evening the mood was melancholy. It was the same with other "last nights" on past trips and I would find it to be true with most future trips. Perhaps it was a combination of things. Fatigue, alcohol, pot, diminished adrenalin, and the stark realization that we would not do this for at least another year.

We cooked steaks, finished the beans, drank a few beers and were in bed before eleven. The following morning we were up early. We packed the cars and decided to stop for breakfast on the way home.

Prior to leaving, however, I felt the urge to return to the bathroom. I perched on the toilet and surveyed the room. It was unusual in that I had never seen a larger bathroom in my life. It appeared to be out of character with the rest of the old farmhouse. This room had obviously been recently remodeled. In addition to a double sink and vanity, there was an antique, free-standing tub. There was a separate shower and a large cupboard in the corner. The wainscoted walls were painted white and the floor was newly laid traditional black and white linoleum. It was the corner cupboard, however, that drew my attention. It extended from the floor almost to the ceiling. It wasn't the size, shape or workmanship that intrigued me. It was the scratching coming from inside the cupboard. Something obviously wanted to get out.

I called out to Bob and he entered the bathroom.

"There's something in that cupboard." I told him.

"What is it?" he asked.

"Bob, look at me. I'm sitting on the fuckin' toilet. I am in the middle of taking a shit. I tell you there is something in the cupboard and you ask me what it is? The reason I called your raunchy ass in here is so that you might help me discover what is in the cupboard."

Bob grinned good-naturedly and moved toward the cupboard. The scratching persisted. I don't know what I thought might be in that cupboard. I don't know why I didn't wait until I finished taking a shit to investigate. When Bob opened the cupboard, a rat the size of a football started to tumble out. Bob reacted quickly and shut the cupboard door. All I had seen was its furry, plump body half-wedged in the cupboard door. My overwhelming urge was to get off that toilet and get out of that bathroom but I couldn't. Nature was persistent, I looked up at Bob with my shorts around my ankles. His hand was still resting on the cupboard door. The rat was in a frenzy, only inches away. Bob was beaming. I knew that grin, but now there was a glint in his eye. I knew exactly what he was thinking. My hand reached for the tissue, but I didn't take my eyes off Bob.

"Bob," I said as calmly as I could. "If you open that cupboard I will have to kill you."

The seconds ticked away and I could sense the battle taking place in Bob's mind. Finally, he moved away from the cupboard, still chuckling. I sighed with relief, finished my business and gratefully left the bathroom.

The ride home was in contrast to the ride up. Instead of animated conversation, there was mostly silence. I observed Maypo driving the truck. Nobody was drinking beer. Bob's shaggy head of blond curls were splayed against the passenger side window. I was quite sure he was sleeping.

Maypo on Rendezvous

"All are lunatics, but he who can analyze his delusions is called a philosopher.

AMBROSE BIERCE

AUGUSTA

I AM IN MY old journals now, leathery, beaten notebooks I carried around for years. They range from poems to scrawl, story ideas to drawings of naked women. They remind me that I went a few places, saw some things, and lacked the discipline to write. But the journals have great value here because the scribbled pages contain notes for every Big Blue trip I went on.

In June of 1976, two cars and a pick-up truck buzzed up the Maine turnpike. Sausage drove the Fishmobile, a white Ford Fairlane with a swooped hind quarter. It got its name after a package of cod slipped out of a grocery bundle and rotted under the front seat. The stench never aired out and tree deodorizers were permanently hung on the window cranks. The Fishmobile started to sputter and Sausage swung into the breakdown lane for a pit stop. He popped the hood, diagnosed an over-heated distributor cap, and emptied a can of cold beer on it. Not a factory recommended procedure, but it worked, and it seemed fitting that the car responded to beer as much as we did at 10 in the morning.

Buck, the strong, quiet, slippery one, was under the influence and anxious to test out the front wheel drive of his new Audi sedan. A 70-foot embankment ran up on the side of the freeway and Buck pointed his shiny, black beauty toward it. The front bumper bit turf at the start of the climb and, for a moment, Buck questioned his assault on the 45° wall. Then he went for it, which was the Big Blue way, and powered up 50 feet of harsh angle before his front wheels spun into submission.

A rock on the home front, a pillar of the community, Buck seldom got out and Big Blue trips were his license to fly. He revved the motor hard and dug holes with his front wheels before rolling back down to road level.

Big Tom, Buck's father-in-law, a Korean war vet, got out of his pick-up truck and came running.

"Buck, Buck, what are you doing?"

"Checking the traction, Tom" Buck replied, as if any prudent traveler might do the same.

Big Tom had never seen the wild side of Buck. He trusted him with his only daughter and thought Buck could do no wrong, but here on the side of Route 95, within eyeshot of the last tollbooth, Buck had pulled a reckless maneuver. Big Tom walked back to his truck, talking to himself the whole way. We knew it was risky taking the big guy on a Blue Trip. He was old school, which put him at odds with several members of our troop.

There was Van, my college roommate, with his blond hair halfway down his back. There was Lyle, with his afro and bag of red Columbo. Bobby, of course, the ultimate bohemian, me with my notebook of poetry, and Whippo, a Doctor of Philosophy who used Socratic method on non-students. Buck asked us to tread softly around Big Tom. For all his physical strength, his ego was fragile.

Big Tom's education was cut short by the Korean war where he patrolled the front lines in machine gun jeeps and excelled in hand-to-hand combat. He worked in cement after the war and hardened to Hulk-like proportions at 5'10, 245 pounds. He loved being the center of attention, cracking jokes and punching you in the shoulder. Due to hearing loss from machine-gun fire, his misnomers were hilarious. The pain in his legs resulted from "very close veins" and the North Carolina airport he flew to was "Wally Durham." No matter what Tom said, he needed to know you were laughing with him, not at him.

We flew up the north way to Augusta where Bobby had a friend who agreed to rent us the family "camp." We were cruising past Portland at 75 mph when a chopper motored along in the passing lane. The driver sported a leather flight helmet and goggles. The passenger was skinny and strung out. They looked like Cheech and Chong after an all-night bender in which they accidentally drank the contents of their water-pipe.

The bikers came alongside Buck's Audi and Van offered them a Bud out the window. They nabbed the all-American brew and came in for another. Then Lyle took the camaraderie a step further. He lit a joint, stretched his long arm out the window, and offered the blazing spleef. Chong snagged it cleanly, completing the fastest open-air pass in Big Blue history. The bikers pressed on, toking and drinking their way up the freeway. We passed a sign: Maine - the way it's supposed to be. I'm not sure this is what they had in mind.

We were becoming a Society at that point. We had a mission, a purpose, even a motto - Go For It. What we lacked was an initiation rite, something that would set us apart. Sausage, Bobby, and I put our warped minds together came up with a little something for Dr. Whippo based on Bobby's role in the Society.

"Just a head's up, Whippo," I said. "We have an initiation right. Tell him, Bob."

Bobby angled to Whippo in the back seat. "Have you ever been with a man?"

"In the biblical sense?"

"Ah-huh."

"Of course not."

"That'll change," Bob said. "Somewhere, sometime on this trip, I'm going to hit you in the seat."

Bob kept a straight face. We all did. Whippo looked about, threw back a beer and cracked another.

"Right," he said.

We said nothing. In the silence that ensued, Whippo had to wonder what he'd gotten himself into. Surely we were pulling his leg, we were straight rangers, but there was something unsettling about the Bobman. He was capable of anything.

"It's not something we do all the time," Sausage said, "only on Rendezvous, and you're sworn to secrecy on this. It goes no further than the guys on this trip, and Big Tom's out. He wouldn't understand. But you're our brother-in-law, and you've got a right to know. Bob's a fudge-packer and so am I."

It caught Whippo mid-swig. Beer shot out his nose and he coughed from his gut-hunks. Bob gave his knee a reassuring pat, and Whippo slapped it away. It was going to be a long trip for the good doctor.

Bobby's friend, Burnsy, lived with his mother in a quiet, fenced neighborhood. Our caravan pulled into his driveway and Burnsy surveyed the lot of us. Sausage poured another beer on his distributor cap. Lyle cleared empties from the front seat of Buck's car. Buck revved his engine. Big Tom checked the lashings on his canoe, and Whippo wandered toward the hedge. I think Burnsy was having second thoughts about renting us the family camp.

Bursy and Bob had served together in Nam and met up at Disabled American Veterans conventions. Bursy's wounds were not obvious, but he had them.

"It's just a camp," Burnsy said, pulling the keys out of his pocket, "but it means a lot to us."

"We'll take care of it like it's our own," Bobby promised.

He reached for the keys and Burnsy held them back.

"Who's the prick pissing on the hedge?"

Bobby turned and saw Whippo relieving himself in full view of the house across the street.

"That's Doctor Whippo. He teaches at the college."

"You'd think he'd know better."

"And you'd be wrong."

"Tell him to keep it in his pants. You can get arrested for that kind of thing up here."

Burnsy handed over the keys and we were on our way, bounding down a dirt road through a field and bottoming out in ruts. Sausage told Bobby to slow down, and Bobby laughed. He'd driven jeeps in the jungles of Nam. The Fishmobile on a cart trail was a piece of cake.

The Burns family camp was nestled under tall pines by a bend in the Kennebec River. We parked the cars roadside and made our way down to the lap-board cottage. The wrap-around deck offered commanding views of a pond in the river. Horse pits complimented the front yard, and a long dock was capped with a 15-foot diving tower. It was perfect for 5 days of fun and frolic.

The cabin had an open floor plan thoughtfully appointed with hunting-motif sofas, easy chairs, and army-issue cots. A ladder led to additional sleeping quarters in the loft, and the kitchen was tight but tidy. The air smelled of Pinesol and the floors glowed as only old pine can. We dropped our duffels, broke out cheap cigars, and made ourselves right at home.

A canoe floated past on Big Tom's shoulders. A serious angler, he had a bead on the Big Blue pot. While still on the dock, he caught his first fish and called to Buck.

"Buck, Buck, that's one!" Big Tom boomed.

We were all enthused, but as the day wore on Tom's call went out so many times, it took an extraordinary effort on Buck's part to even nod. At which point, Tom added an airhorn.

"Buck, that's a dozen!" (honk)!

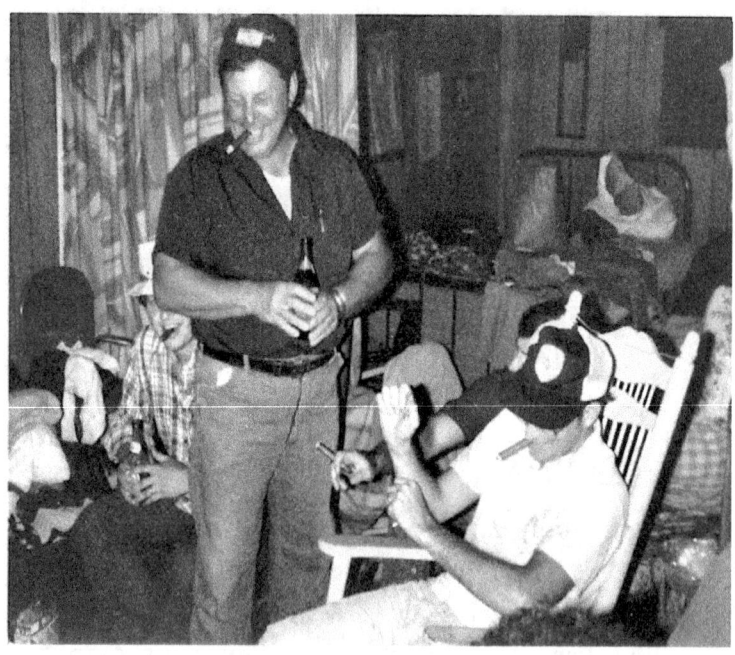

Big Tom cutting up

Buck felt the need to apologize. "Sorry guys, he begged to come. Literally pleaded. How do you say no to that?"

One advantage to Big Tom out on the water is we could smoke weed up on the deck. Back then, marijuana was a Schedule 1 drug, right up there with LSD, Quaaludes, Heroin and Peyote. Possession in amounts over an ounce could earn you jail time because no one in their right mind would have an ounce for personal consumption. Defacto, you were a dealer. So it was back then, and Tom was dead against weed.

Van broke some buds and rolled an Esmerelda. For those not familiar with this form of smoking pleasure, it was 10-inch-long joint swaddled with special papers. Van was a master and produced one so even and full, it rivaled a high-end cigar. We spread out on the deck and passed it around for the better part of an hour.

Whippo by the loft

When nothing particular was going on, the initiation rite would rear its head. Bobby would blow Whippo a secretive kiss. I'd give him a slow wink. Sausage would say, "Whip's looking sweet." Buck would confide, "Bobby made a man out of me."

Whippo tried to brush it off, but we were getting to him. When night came down, he set his cot between Big Tom and the wall, far from Bobby's perch in the loft. He zipped his sleeping bag up to his chin and insisted the kitchen light be left on.

"Goodnight Whippo," Bobby whispered from above.

"Fertigate zich," Whippo said, resorting to German.

"What's going on?" Big Tom asked.

"Bob's sweet on Whippo," Sausage said.

"It's his mind he really wants to fuck," Buck added.

Guys live like slobs when women aren't around. Beer cans crowd window ledges, cigarette butts overflow ashtrays, dishes fester in the sink, and orderly quarters turn into a pigsty. Bobby was at the heart of it as he was with so many things. In his mind, a Rendezvous was a chance to leave the trappings of civilization behind, and that included hygiene. No duffel accompanied him on this trip, not even a toothbrush. He wore a plaid shirt, blue jeans, presumably underwear, and moccasins flattened to triple E. That was his wardrobe for the week. On the 3rd day, Sausage offered him a change of clothes.

"I'm just getting comfy in these," Bobby said.

Multiple days of fishing, drinking, horse-shoe tournaments, over-eating, skinny-dipping, and cannabis abuse left us sated. Lyle mistook it for malaise and decided to rally the troops. He cracked open a handle of Canadian Club and took long, straight gulps. It was barely noon.

"He's going for it," Buck said.

That was an understatement.

When Lyle drinks, he transforms from a thoughtful individual into a wild man. In the early going, he'll be standing next to you, lose his balance, right himself with a side-step, and act like his equilibrium is not shot. The more he drinks, the more he tries to act like he's sober, and strong drink puts him over the edge. The ground moves under his feet, roots rise to trip, trees jump in his way, and there is no straight line between two points. Toward the end of bender, you'll find him on the outskirts of a conversation, eyes half-shut, bottom lip heading for his chin. You'll says something to him and his head will bob, that's all he can muster.

I saw him going hard at the whisky and took the bottle from him around mid-afternoon. He staggered after me across the deck, put his foot through a soft board and sank up to his thigh. The guys rolled as Lyle wriggled free and came after me again, taking vain swipes at the bottle.

"Okay, Maypo, you dink, you fucking dink. Down to the pit. We'll settle this mono e mono."

He thumped his chest and swaggered off, bumping off deck chairs and into railings like a pinball. The hole in the deck lay ahead.

"Watch that step," Buck said.

Lyle turned and pointed in the Buck's general direction. "You're fucking next," he said.

"You talking to me?" Big Tom asked.

"No, the fat fuck Buck."

Lyle stumbled down the stairs and weaved his way to the horse-pits. I turned to the guys for guidance.

"He called you a dink," Big Tom said.

"A fucking dink," Sausage added.

I felt the need to defend myself, but Lyle was my best friend, and we never had a cross word in our lives. But here, in the rare air of a Big Blue Rendezvous, we were about to come to blows. It was not my idea of a good time.

"Don't hurt him," Buck said, "just put him in line."

I took a pull off the whiskey and went to confront Lyle. The guys gathered at the railing like it was a school yard fight. Lyle did his version of the Ali shuffle, fell off kilter and reared up like an old-time boxer with his dukes up.

I grabbed him by the shirt. "Lyle, I don't want to hit you."

His shoulders sank and the bravado fell. 80 proof vapors hit me in the face. "Maypo, you know you'd kick… my… ass."

Lyle didn't want to fight; he wanted to get my goat. I pushed him back and he fell like a tower of cookies. The guys straggled from the railing, and I saw myself in that moment as a dink, a fucking dink.

"That'll learn you," Lyle yowled after me, "Don't ever shut me off."

I hit the bottle hard after that.

⚬

Journal extract, June 29th, 1976:

I'm in the outhouse, fending off mosquitoes, taking a crap. Bobby's on the porch, singing his version of "We're Not Going To Take It" by The Who:

"Welcome to the camp, I guess you all know why you're here

My name is Bobby and I became aware this year…"

He chuckles to himself. My head throbs, eardrums quiver.

"How ya doing, Maypo?" Bob asks.

"Pretty shitty." The damn truth.

⚬

We developed a code for getting stoned when Big Tom was around. Someone would say, "I'm going to check on the cars," and several guys would go roadside to toke. At first, Big Tom thought nothing of it, but the call went out so often, Tom asked if the cars were safe. One day, he decided to check on them himself and caught Van blowing a joint. He was ready to call the cops, but Buck talked him out of it. He said it would ruin the trip.

"You keep that shit away from my Buck," Big Tom told Van, "or so help me God, I'll break you in two."

Big Tom literally could, and Van knew it. All the same, he didn't put the joint out. He waited until Big Tom was out of sight and toked it to the nib.

Later, Van succumbed to the munchies, and Tom caught him eating ice-cream directly out of a half-gallon container, Tom's half-gallon container. Van had spent a year in a lumberjack camp where guys lived together and ate 7-day stew. This trip seemed as communal as that. He said he would replace the ice cream. Tom took him up on it, and those were the last words between them on this trip.

We went on an ice-cream run looking rough. We needed a shower, a shave and, in Bobby's case, a whole new wardrobe. Lyle went to get beer while Sausage, Bobby, Buck and I hit the local Newport Creamery. We sat at the counter and a pretty girl came to take our order. Sausage sprung for a banana split, Bobby wanted a cone of coffee, I got a milkshake, and Buck ordered off the menu.

"I'll have a bumblast," he said.

"E-excuse me?" the girl stammered.

"A bumblast," Buck repeated like it was clearly on the menu and wholly in the realm of possibility.

The girl blushed and tapped her pencil on her pad. Bobby and I cracked up. The cook turned from the burgers on his grill.

"He'll have a hot-fudge sundae," Sausage said, closing Buck's menu.

"With cream and nuts?" the waitress asked, avoiding eye-contact with Buck. The question hung in the air for an extra second or two.

"Sure," Sausage said.

The waitress hustled off to fill our order. She whispered to an older girl, who looked at Buck. He was so handsome, I believe she considered honoring his request.

"Bumblast" is a strange word. It originated in the Sullivan family when someone found a pair of underwear that looked like a shotgun blew out the back side. We hung them on a trophy and gave it out as a dubious achievement award. Here, in this innocent creamery, the word popped out of Buck's mouth. While it's meaning was unclear, it conjured pleasures of a nether sort.

The cook came out of the kitchen, wiping his hands on his

greasy apron. He was a big fellar with arms that needed hairnets. He checked with the girls to see if everything was ok, and they said it was. All the same, the cook kept a close eye on us as our waitress served the ice-cream. She set the sundae before Buck, hastily. He looked at it, disappointed.

"That's not a bumblast."

Bob once said that Buck had more pure craziness than the rest of his brothers put together. It tended to come out on Rendezvous.

The girl returned to her station and busied herself wiping counters. The cook went back to his burgers but watched us between flips. We ate our ice-cream, picked up Big Tom's half gallon, and left without further incident.

"We can't be doing this," Sausage said as we went out the door. "We can't be around people on Rendezvous."

In the parking lot, Lyle was pushing the envelope of propriety a step further. He had five cases of beer stacked on the Fishmobile's hood and was propped against the windshield with Sausage's drill sergeant hat atop his afro. Hendrix throbbed from the stereo to complete the spectacle.

Women with shopping carts told their children to look away. Shop-owners stood in their doorways, gawking. A crew of lumber-jacks pulled in, hauling a woodchipper. We packed the beer in the trunk and Lyle in the car before they could run him through the chipper.

On the last night, Bobby trotted out his culinary skills and made American chop suey. There was no pan big enough for his three pounds of shells and four pounds of meat sauce so he mixed his batch in the refrigerator crisper drawer. He set in on the stove and brought it to a simmer.

"Damn, that smells good," Whippo said.

"I hope you like it," Bob said, sweet as pie.

I took the remains of the Canadian Club and climbed to the top of the diving tower. Fifteen feet above the Kennebec River, I wrote what was adopted as...

The Anthem of the Blues

What might possess a man
to let the shit hit the fan
to leave behind a house and wife
and pursue an uncommon life?
What might possess a man
to take up life's trash can
fill it full of ice and brew
and tell the fucking world to screw?
Most are not as bold as these
they wear their balls in parentheses
they suck scumbags and shoot the breeze
they spend their lives on their knees.
But life is full of niggly shit
the chores and bores where you do your bit
to make the world a better place
and save the blasted human race.
In the end, the good man outs
the straitjacket breaks, the spirit shouts,
"Smoke your pot and swill your booze,
the Big Blues have paid their dues."

Night came down and the guys crashed out. Bobby made his way up the ladder and sat on his cot. He had gained seven pounds in five days and his belly was enormous. He hunked it together around his scar that ran from sternum to pubes, making a hairy cleft.

"Don't you want to fuck that, Maypo."

Bob was incorrigible.

"Hey Lyle," he called down as the guys were crawling into their sacks, "Are you going to rehab when you get back?"

Lyle mumbled something. He hadn't regained his form after the day of whiskey.

"You could sell your liver to science," Sausage suggested.

"Yeah, yeah," Lyle muttered.

The guys were tired and so were the jokes. Buck asked what time we were leaving in the morning. Sausage said he was heading back early. No sense hanging around. The party was over. A major clean-up had to be done, but we'd face that in the morning.

Night came down and farts mixed with the chorus of bullfrogs outside. Lyle started to snore, and others were nodding off.

"Maypo," Bobby whispered, "the time has come."

Below, snug in his sack, lay Whippo. He rested easy now, confident that he had passed the test. It was all a ruse; Bobby was not going to hit him in the seat. But the Bobman had other plans. He climbed over the railing and took aim at his prey. Whippo lay his cot, hands over his chest, glasses on the side table. All was still when Bob let out a call that shook the rafters.

"Whippo, Bobby wants you!"

He dove a full twelve feet through the air and body-slammed the shuddering philosopher below. The army cot splintered beneath them and Whippo screamed, "No!" and "Don't!"

Big Tom turned on the light. "What the hell's going on?"

Bobby rolled off Whippo, convulsing in laughter that brought no sound. We were all caught in the grip of that silence, laughing so hard tears came to our eyes. Whippo picked himself off the floor, mumbling something no one could hear. He gathered his sleeping bag, torn by the cot rail, and climbed to the loft, dropping wadding the whole way.

Big Tom held up the cot rail that was sharp as a bayonet. "Someone could get hurt doing stuff like that."

Whippo sat on a cot in the corner of the loft. He popped a beer, looked at me, and shook his head. Whippo had been had.

Later, after things calmed down, Bobby called up sweetly. "Did you like it?"

"Fick dich," Whippo cursed, auf Deutsch.

"He liked it," Bobby cooed.

We laughed well into the night. As sleep grazed our temples, someone would snort and we'd be rolling again. Whippo fell asleep sitting up, beer in hand, bathed in the glare of a bare bulb. He was 37, the father of 4, a respected professor, and now a full-fledged member of the Big Blue.

We broke camp early. Sausage was anxious to get home, and Buck couldn't wait to take a shower. He felt "skeevy," but Bobby gave new meaning to the word. His clothes bore every smear of mustard, blot of ketchup and slime of worm. That was on the outside. From within, a putrid odor radiated. He passed with a ripe bag of garbage, and I wasn't sure what smelled worse, Bobby or the trash.

"Bob, why didn't you bring a change of clothes?" I asked.

"Maypo, when you set an ambush in Nam, you dig yourself a hole and sit there for hours. You have to take a piss, and you can't go find yourself a tree, so you piss your pants and deal with it. When you've lived like that for years, what's a little ketchup or grease?"

We ditched the broken cot in a crawl space under the cabin and put a board over the hole Lyle stomped through the deck. There was nothing we could do about the broken lamp or torn window screen. Burnsy made a mistake and he'd have to accept it. But the crisper drawer was another matter. Bobby knew that the chop suey annealed to the white porcelain would bother Burnsy. He took it out back, found a leafy spot, and used it to dig its own hole. Bobby had buried things before and they told no tales.

The guys went back to their respective lives. Sausage, Buck, and Bobby became proud fathers that year. Whippo chaired the Humanities Department at the college. Big Tom took his wife to Florida to "break up the monogamy." Van moved to Oregon and we never heard from him again. Lyle got an English degree and went to work in an art foundry. I went to graduate school for film studies. Ten years would pass before the Society came together for another Rendezvous.

From time to time, Bob runs into Burnsy at a D.A.V. convention. It's been many years since we stayed at the camp, but Burnsy still asks about the crisper drawer.

"What could have happened to a crisper drawer?"

Bobby has no idea.

Lyle choosing tackle

Nothing so fortifies a friendship as a belief on the part of one friend that he is superior to the other.

HONORÉ DE BALZAC

SCOUTS

WHILE SAUSAGE, BUCK, Bobby and Whippo were tied down taking care of small children, Lyle and I went in search of a place where the Society could cut loose and not worry about contact with the outside world. The Adirondacks caught our eye and we set out as scouts.

In late June, 1977, Lyle and I scored an ounce of black, opiated hash, and set sail for Lake Placid, New York. Lyle had been there as a kid and remembered it was a sleepy lakeside village. We pulled into town well after midnight and it was nothing like Lyle remembered. The Winter Olympics had come to Lake Placid and it looked like a tourist trap.

We pressed on. I was exhausted from 8 hours behind the wheel and the roadway was turning into freeze frames… which meant I was falling asleep with my eyes open. Imaginary creatures crossed the road and I hit the brakes several times. Lyle offered to drive, but he was clearly intoxicated.

"This is nuts," I said. "We don't know where we are, we don't know where we're going, you're drunk, and I'm fucking hallucinating."

"Ain't it great," Lyle said.

We passed a sign for the Trudeau Institute, which had been a Sanatorium during the Tuberculosis epidemic. I was ready to check into one of the lakeside cottages.

"Stop the car!" Lyle shouted, staring into the maw of darkness out the passenger window.

I wheeled onto the soft shoulder and dropped my head to the steering wheel. Lyle stumbled down the embankment and I assumed it was another piss stop. Moments later, he appeared in my headlights, motioning me off the road like a Keystone cop. He guided me to the entrance of an abandoned road, and I squeezed my car between a boulder and a tree. Lyle hopped in and we were on our way, bounding through the woods on a trail that looked like the fire-roads around the Swansicut Reservoir. The mystery trip came to a sudden end in a cul-de-sac about a half mile into the woods. That was good enough for me. I cut the engine, reclined my seat, and fell asleep. More precisely, I passed out.

In the morning, I woke to the sound of beer cans tumbling out the passenger door. I cracked one eye and saw Lyle amble off into the woods. I fell into a dream about a student in my history class that I had no right dreaming about and woke to the sound of Lyle hauling his cooler out of the trunk.

"Wake up, Maypo. We fucking found it!"

Lyle opened the glovebox and nabbed the hash.

"Where are you going with that?"

Lyle smiled like the Cheshire Cat and hatted off into the woods. Two things crossed my mind: Lyle could blow through hash faster than a blast furnace, and what had we found? I gave chase.

These were big woods, dominated by giant hemlocks and carpeted with legions of moss. Rills trickled from beneath boulders and tracts of balsam scented the air. It was not the oak and pine forests of the Swansicut. These were alpine woods where the short growing season called everything to sudden and startling life.

I moshed through a fern gully and caught sight of Lyle vanishing in a hollow. He was galumphing with a full cooler of beer, moving fast. Excitement prickled my skin as I broke out of the forest into a clearing.

A dilapidated cabin stood at the edge of dawn struck waters. The screens were bashed out, the shingles cupped, the door angled off its hinges. It bore a sign identifying it as belonging to State of New York on a 99-year lease, a lease that had run out. Lyle's cooler was on the front step, and he was crossing a plank to a boulder capped by a wrought iron bench. We were in a cove shrouded in mist. As the sun crested the mountains, pockets of mist waltzed like Djinn and rose into the sky.

"Am I fucking good or what?" Lyle said.

I had to hand it to him; Lyle had found it. We didn't know it was Lower Saranac Lake and we were in Lonesome Bay. We didn't know that camping was permitted all around the lake, but strictly forbidden in this cove. We didn't know the 30-inch pike patrolled the shore and bears owned the woods. All we knew was that opiated hash could fuck you up and leave you watching water bugs for hours.

"What time do you think it is?" Lyle asked.

"Ten-thirty, maybe 11."

Lyle eyed the sky. "It's 1:15."

He said it with such surety that I had to debate. Eventually, I walked back to the car to prove him wrong, but Lyle was right, within minutes of the hour. It was uncanny, considering the time-distorting properties of black hash. And this time-check conversation repeated itself over and over. I began to wonder why time was so important to Lyle. We had six unscheduled days and he was marking the hour. Was he pitting my internal clock against his? If so, it was competition, and Lyle and I went at it head to head.

From an early age, we were blessed with an opponent who refused to put the gauntlet down. Skipping stones, swimming laps, holding our breath, ping-pong, whatever, we were out to prove who was best. I had him in hockey, and Lyle could eat my lunch in hoops. For the rest, we were dead even. Someday, we'd be a couple old farts in a nursing home seeing who could go faster in a platform rocker.

We pitched my cabin tent with the door facing the fire and the lake beyond. We set out sleeping bags, gathered wood and cooked sausages with sides of bacon and potato. Many beers and joints later, we retired to the tent expecting a good night's sleep. Wrong for me. Lyle snored like a dying man on a respirator. Every few minutes, the respirator shut off and Lyle stopped breathing. Twenty seconds of silence would ensue and then Lyle would gasp awake only to snore again moments later. It was impossible to sleep within a hundred feet of Lyle. I resolved to get separate tents in the future.

After midnight, I heard something big coming through the woods. Limbs broke off trees, branches snapped on the ground. I shook Lyle hard and pulled him up to a sitting position.

"Wha?" he asked, unable to complete the word.

"Listen," I said in a hush.

His eyes were at half mast, his senses dulled by drugs and sleep. He could not hear what sounded like a Hummer bashing toward us through the woods. He fell back down, and I pulled him up again. Now he was pissed.

"What?!"

I put a finger to my lips and pointed out the door. There was a half-moon that night, enough light to see the world outside. Fifteen feet away, the fire pit smoldered, a thin stream of smoke wafting from where Lyle poured his bacon grease. He loved the way it flared up and scented the air with traces of hickory. I could smell it now. It was on us, on our clothes.

A dark form broke into the clearing, menacing on all fours, head going side to side. Ursus Americanus, the American Black Bear, second only to Polar Bears in unprovoked attacks on humans. They tended to rend and maul for the sport of it. Lyle and I had rung the dinner bell but left the table bare.

The bear dug morsels of steak fat out of the campfire and licked at the spot where Lyle dumped his grease. Then it rose up and inventoried the site with his snout. He smelled us right down to the Slim Jims in my pocket. Lucky for us, he went after our trash. After a huge ruckus, the bear left, and Lyle went back to snoring. I lay there too frightened to sleep.

In the morning, Lyle said there was no bear. He remembered me waking him up and freaking out about something, again. He saw nothing, heard nothing. The torn-up trash… probably a raccoon.

I showed him paw print the size of my hand. Lyle studied it.

"Huge racoon," he said, busting my chops.

All the same, he dumped his bacon grease on the fire.

"What are you thinking, Lyle?"

"I'm not thinking, Maypo. Get off my case."

I figured we'd see the bear again that night.

Lyle and I took a swim and sat on the bench. We toked hash and watched the water bugs bump into one another. A couple hours later, we came out of the trance.

"Lyle, you know that girl in my history class?"

"The one who never crosses her legs?"

"Yeah."

"The one with the nips that poke through her shirt?"

"Yeah, Lyle…"

"The one who flares her nostrils at you?"

"Lyle, I'm trying to tell you something…"

"Just making sure I had the right one. What about her?"

"What should I do?"

"How old is she?"

"Seventeen."

"Eighteen's the magic number."

"I know, I know. I'd lose my job, my fiancée, probably face charges, and for what? A hot affair with a precocious teen… sneaking around, hotel sex, car sex, ponytail bobbing—"

"Ok, ok, get to the point."

I looked out over the water. The lake was so stunning and pure, all I needed was to come here once a year.

"I'm gonna pass," I said. "I'm not going for it."

Lyle assessed my resolve and looked away. "Maybe I should get into teaching."

A green power boat entered the cove and came our way. Not a pleasure craft, it was captained by a gray-haired forest ranger who guided it expertly to our rock.

"You can't camp here," he said.

My heart sank. I felt like paradise was being snatched away.

"But there's camping all around the lake. Boat access only."

"We don't have a boat," Lyle pointed out.

"I see that. Well, Walt Thompson can hook you up down in Ampersand Bay."

We broke camp and drove to Walt Thompsons's Marina on the northeast shore of the lake. Walt was a whiskered old gent who wore suspenders and tended to spit before he spoke. He rented us a 19-foot Grumman canoe made of the same riveted aluminum they put into W.W.II fighter planes. Walt's wife gave us a map and told us to hustle it up.

"Storm's blowing in," she said.

To the west, dark clouds rolled over Ampersand Mountain. Lyle and I packed our canoe and had barely six inches of freeboard on the side. Lyle sat in the bow and pulled long steady strokes. I doubled timed in the back, anxious to make Eagle Island a mile away.

We cleared the mouth of Ampersand Bay and a strong wind hit us in the face. The lake started to pitch and reel, and we had our hands full keeping the canoe going straight. A few degrees off and we'd spin around. I called for Lyle to stroke harder. Instead, he put his paddle down, reached around in the cooler and fished out a beer. We turned 360's and the wind blew us back hundreds of feet.

"Fuck, Lyle, come on!"

"Yeah, yeah," he said, getting back to work.

Lightning flashed over Ampersand Mountain and thunder rolled. If we were caught on the open water in an electrical storm, the canoe would act as a lightning rod. I stroked like hell and the rain came, stinging my face. White caps crashed the bow and water raced over the gunwales. Lyle was into it now, his long arms stabbing the water and leaving it behind. We fought for the Sister Islands and dove under the cover of a white cedar. Lightning jagged from the sky and gales tore down the lake. Had we been out in the full force of it, we would have gone down.

The storm passed and we made camp on Eagle Island, soaked but grateful. There was a picnic table, a fire pit, and an outhouse. The State of New York described the camping facilities as "primitive," but it was all the Society would need. We couldn't wait to tell them about our find.

It rained that night, all the next day, and the day after. Lyle and I spent long hours in our tent, playing cards, drinking beer and staying stoned. We hadn't checked the weather report and it wouldn't have mattered because our week of vacation was set. Despite the foul weather, we had a blast. We couldn't cook, so Lyle ate tuna out of the can with a dollop of mayo on top. I was down to hotdogs which I rationalized were fully cooked.

During breaks in the downpours, Lyle would look to west and say it was clearing. We would build a roaring fire, toss in potatoes wrapped in tin foil, prep our sausages, and then the rains would come. At one point we retreated to the cover a boulder that had a slight overhang. We stood under it and watched our fire turn to a puddle. Lyle opened another can of tuna. I ate a half-baked potato. The misadventure is the adventure, or so it was for us.

On the last night, the rain stopped. Everything was drenched, but Lyle's waterproof matches came through. We built a roaring fire, hung everything up to dry, and put on the last of our food: a huge can of Dinty Moore beef stew. Our ice was gone, our beer cooled in the lake, and we discussed improvements to our camping experience: more ice, separate tents, proper tarping. We could have added cooking to the list.

Set directly on the coals, the can of Dinty Moore was expanding and contracting, pulsing in place. The sidewalls rippled at the seams and the lid bulged.

"Did you punch a hole in the top?" I asked.

"I thought you did."

Before we could release the pressure, the can exploded, spraying the campsite with bits of beef, potato and carrot. That was our dinner for the night. I found a chunk of potato impaled on a broken branch and ate it. It tasted good.

We broke camp early in the morning. The hash was gone, the coolers empty, and we had work the next day. It was perfect weatherwise, and we griped about leaving, but we'd come back, hopefully with the Society.

On our way to Ampersand Bay, we scouted sites and Green Island stood out. It was a large island with a single campsite perched at the edge of an outcrop. A flat rock at shore level would make an ideal place to land boats, swim and bask in the sun. We took note and filed it for our Big Blue report.

When we got to Walt Thompson's place, Lyle called for a final time check. I guessed it was 9:15. He said it was 10:37. I was miserable with his week-long pronouncements and ducked into the car to prove him wrong. But Lyle was right, down to the minute.

"How do you fucking do that?"

He pulled a small Timex out of his breast pocket and dangled it before me. "It's easy when you have a watch."

Alcohol loosens the tongue and tightens the bonds of friendship.

ANONYMOUS

THE FIRST MEETING

IN THE YEARS following our trip to the Augusta, Bobby, Sausage, Buck and Whippo dove into family life with the same gusto they mustered for the 15-foot tower at the Burns Camp. Here's a brief update on the members and why they couldn't go on a Rendezvous.

Bobby was living in a quiet suburb of Concord, New Hampshire, with his beautiful wife and two rapscallion boys he called Hammer and Spike. He was working out of a DAV field office, driving a red, white, and blue van to the small towns, reaching out to vets. It put him in touch with guys who needed better services, more compensation, and fair treatment. When he was not on the road, he coached Little League and joined the board of the Concord Youth Baseball Association. He carried a clipboard around when he coached and, if someone complained, he handed it to them.

"What's this?" they'd ask.

"Sign-up sheet for the Board of Directors."

"I don't want to serve on the Board."

"Neither do I," Bobby would say.

It always ended the discussion.

Sausage was working at Sullivan Sand and Gravel, heading up the operation along with Buck, and consulting with our father on major decisions. The company was at a crossroad. The gravel bank had been eaten to the borders and there was no material left to support the building boom in the Northeast. Sausage came up with the idea of transforming Sullivan Sand and Gravel into a ready-mix concrete company. They invested in a fleet of cement trucks and shipped concrete all over the state. When Sausage was not quoting jobs, he hosted backyard barbecues with Crash and drove his three daughters to activities. On the side, he took banjo lessons from Shitfish and taught catechism at the church.

Buck was raising 3 boys with the firm hand and patient understanding that our father showed us. He didn't want his sons to grow up in the shadow of a big oak, so he cut them slack. His boys ran around naked most of the time and pissed down the air vents for convenience. Buck knew they needed structure and discipline so he got them into youth hockey, a rigorous year-round sport in Rhode Island. He and his wife traveled the boys to rinks all over New England and drank coffee that tasted like it was made from Zamboni melt.

Whippo taught at the college and gained a reputation as one of the sternest instructors to ever walk the halls. Together with my sister, he was raising 2 girls and 2 boys. The girls were easy until they hit puberty, and the boys were a handful from the start. Whippo took a philosophic view of his mischievous sons: they were naturals for the Society.

Lyle and I held bachelor quarters on the 1st floor of a tenement house and our fiancées lived on the 3rd floor. I was teaching at a public high school, Lyle was working at the art foundry, and things were going swimmingly until Lyle's fiancé gave him an ultimatum. He took the plunge, I followed, and we were on our way to becoming family guys.

It was the best of days for these fine young men, and the worst of days for the Big Blue. Fishing trips were on hold, so we settled for an overnight campout. Bobby drove the D.A.V. flagship down from New Hampshire and arrived at Sullivan Sand and Gravel in the late afternoon wearing cut-off jeans and a rugby shirt. He had put on a few pounds since we saw him last and filled out his shirt like an offensive lineman. The cut-offs were another matter.

We had not seen Bobby in shorts since he returned from Vietnam and for good reason. Both shins had fist-size holes that were puffy on the sides, black at the core, and bled from time to time. Bobby kept them out of sight for the most part, but he was letting it all hang out tonight.

"Where are we staying?" Bob asked Sausage.

Sausage handed him a sleeping bag and pointed to the gravel pit. It was an enormous crater with a small, greenish pool at the bottom. Bob asked if it was stocked. Sausage said he was working on it.

We walked to the bottom of the pit and gathered a ring of stones for the fire. The forecast was for a clear night, and we planned to sleep under the stars. Foraging for firewood, we discussed the state of Society.

"Someone needs to take charge," Bob said. "We need a president."

"Who would want to be president of the Big Blue?" Sausage asked. "It's not the kind of thing you put on a resume."

"It's a fucking disgrace," Bobby confirmed, "but someone's got to organize a trip."

"We could elect Whippo," I said, "but he doesn't fish."

"Whippo doesn't get the Big Blue," Bob said, and left it at that.

We kicked around the likes of Lyle, our brother-in-law Dead Eye Mike and Kevin "Cornbread" Feely, the bookkeeper at Sullivan Sand and Gravel, but only one man measured up: Buck. Bobby reasoned that Buck had more trouble getting away than anyone else. If we elected him, he'd succumb to pressure and orchestrate a Rendezvous.

"He'll never fall for it," Sausage said.

"Leave it to me," Bobby replied. "Buck won't know what hit him."

That night Bobby got to Buck. He told him how much the Society meant to him, that he missed seeing his brothers and we needed to go on a fishing trip. The only one who could pull it off was Sausage. Bobby was counting on Buck's vote, and he committed to Bob's plan.

As evening came down, the rest of the guys straggled in. Lyle wore his acid-burned jeans from work and matching denim shirt. Whippo arrived in a pit-stained t-shirt with a stinky cigar clenched between. Dead Eye brought cases of beer and Cornbread brought snacks. We made a fire, roasted hotdogs and had a few rounds. By the time the meeting came to order, a relative term, we were good and tight.

Lyle and I gave our report about Lower Saranac Lake and it sounded great to the guys. Sausage said he would research sites, fees, boat options and licenses, and we could put it all on the company. Buck liked the idea - Sausage was acting presidential.

The election got underway, and two nominees rose to the top: Sausage and Buck. Neither had much of a platform. Sausage said his record spoke for itself, and Buck said he had a dream, but it was a wet one. Votes were cast and it was all even. Bobby held the deciding vote and he ambled around the fire, considering each candidate carefully.

"Don't think too long," Sausage said, worried that Bob might have set him up.

Bob talked about the Big Blue, our origins, and purpose, and how we needed to return to our roots. "Look at us," he said. "We're in a fucking hole and there's not a fish in sight, unless you mean Lyle."

"Blow me," Lyle said.

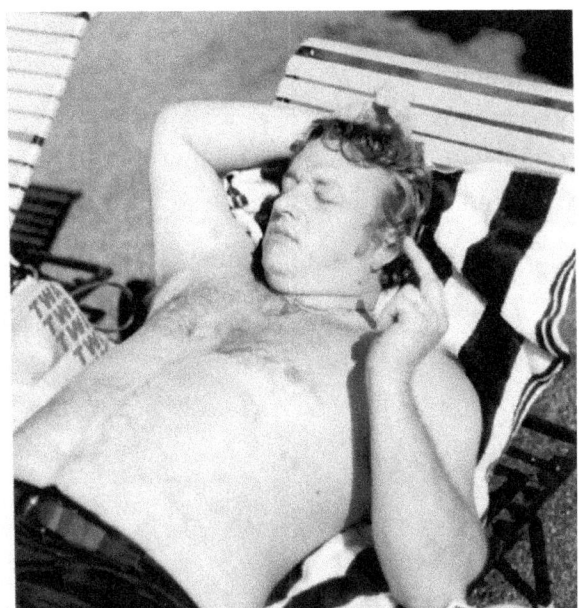

Rigged the first election

Bob winked at Buck. "I'm voting my conscience here, I'm voting for the one man who can put us on track, and that's… Buck."

Buck was dumbfounded. Bob crumbled to the sand, laughing. He'd pulled a fast one and all Buck could do was shake his head.

A few minutes later, Buck gave a rambling acceptance speech. He said he was a sacrificial lamb and, insofar as we had invested him with grave responsibility, he would let us down. He said the Society was a weight on his shoulders and he'd lead by example, a bad one. Then, in a flash of brilliance, he pulled the leg of his Bermuda shorts aside and hung out his dick. He declared that to be the sole right and privilege of office. No one else could hang their dick out their shorts or they'd be up on charges. Buck was clearly the man for the job.

"Point of order," Whippo said.

"What is it?" Buck asked.

"Nothing, Mr. President, I just always wanted to say that."

"I've got a problem," Lyle said, attempting to rise from his cooler only to sit back down.

"Obviously," Sausage quipped.

"Mr. President sounds too formal. How about Grand Puhba."

"We're not the Flintstones, Lyle," Dead Eye said.

First Grand Scrotum

Names were tossed out like Pubic Fester, the Illustrious Shanker, but Dr. Whippo hit upon one that stuck. He bowed to Buck and dubbed him, "The Grand Scrotum."

I took notes on the meeting, but it was hen scrawl. I had quite a buzz going and it felt like we were in a crater on the moon with the stars circling overhead. The fire crackled and our shadows loomed large on the walls, sachems with bull roarers. I was pretty messed up.

Bob dropped in between me and Sausage like a fallen tree. Sometimes the Society felt like a fruiting body on his meaty carcass. Bob had something to say, but I held him off, taking notes.

"Who is this Scribbling Asshole?" Bob asked.

That became my title. Not Secretary, not Mr. Secretary. Scribbling Asshole. About right for the Society.

"I met a girl at a conference in Florida," Bob said. "Her eyes are the color of the ocean. I call her, "Blue.""

"You're married, Bob," Sausage said.

"It's over, Saus."

"You're going to leave you marriage for a girl you just met."

"It's a done deal. That's why I came down. I wanted to tell you guys."

"Bob, let me ask you something," Sausage said. "Does this have anything to do with sex?"

"Absofuckingtively. Blue can suck a tennis ball down fifty feet of garden hose. I can lick my eyebrows and breathe out my ears. We're fucking soul mates."

The fire burned down, and the men crawled into their sacks, all except Bobby who was having a talk with Jack Daniels. He lay on the gravel and broke into a song that combined the Beatles, "A Day in a Life," with fragments from Kris Kristofferson's, "Help Me Make It Through the Night."

He blew his load out in a car
When he got hit right in the jaw
And it felt pretty good
And it ran all down her leg…
I don't know what's right or wrong,
It's just something that looks like porn.

"What the fuck is that?" Sausage asked.

"I don't know," Bob said, "I'm fucking ripped."

In the morning, the sachems were gone, the bull roarers stored away. The sun crested the gravel bank and revealed us for what we were, 7 guys scattered about a burned-out fire like broken points of a compass. There was nothing to do but find our way home, but Bobby wasn't going home. He was moving to Washington and taking a job at the D.A.V. headquarters. Blue would join him there.

"Do me a favor," he said. "Don't tell your mom about the divorce."

Bob hated to let our mom down. She would hear about the

divorce soon enough through the grapevine that connects all women to bad news about men. But Bob's mind was made. He was going for it, same as always.

In the parking lot, we shook hands and Bobby's damaged right thumb came under scrutiny. It was set at a harsh, downward angle like the hammer of a flintlock. When he shook hands, it dug into the soft flesh beside your thumb. Since Bob could shake in no other way, we instituted it as the Big Blue handshake. From that day forward, we all shook the same.

"We're becoming a real society," Buck said.

And we were.

Gentlemen, please accept my resignation. I don't care to belong to any social organization that will accept me as a member.

GROUCHO MARX

INITIATIONS

When it came time to initiate our banjo teacher, Roger Shitfish, and Cornbread Feely, the Bobman was living in Washington, D.C., writing high-powered briefs for the Disabled American Veterans organization. He could not come to the meeting so Buck came up with a little something for the newcomers. **Sausage writes about it** like a guy who enjoys watching other men squirm.

I WAS DEEP IN the woods on a crisp December morning, walking as I did early before work. It was often semi-dark when I left the house and made my way through the orchard to the path that led around the Swansicut Reservoir. After a half hour of brisk walking, the pale winter light glinted through naked tree branches and bounced dully off the water's surface. I reflected on the fact that I hated winter. There was nothing about it that I liked. I missed the energy and promise of new life that comes with spring. I missed the extended daylight of summer and the smells.

In summer when I walked through the orchard, the smell of grass mixed with ripening fruit. In the Fall, when the fruit dropped, the smell was still sweet, but somehow pungent, a harbinger of Winter. On this December morning, the orchard and the woods were bedding down. The absence of leaves allowed sound to travel unmuffled. A rifle shot, perhaps several miles away, echoed in the woods. Dead leaves on the forest floor, bleached of color, looked like discarded pieces of a jigsaw puzzle tossed in frustration.

The smells were changed too. Gone was the sweetness of summer hay and corn. Now dampness and rot competed with each other. Once, on a rare occasion that Bobby discussed his experiences in Nam, he remarked about the smell of death.

"It's kind of a mixture of many odors," he said. "None of them pleasant."

Deeper in the woods, I flushed a deer. He startled me as he scampered off, his white tail bobbing through the bare trees. I watched him until he was gone and fell back into thought. A few days earlier, Maypo had called me with another chapter he wanted me to write. He asked me to recount the meeting that took place back in 1983. Bob was supposed to deliver his Rules of Order. I returned from my walk and called Bob on the phone. I caught him napping on his back porch. He talked about the last chapter he wrote and how he was exhausted. We agreed that Maypo was driving us hard on the Big Blue project. His intensity reminded me of how he had the knack for interrupting a pass in hockey and the rushing like a crazed bull towards the opponent's goal.

"What does he want you to write? Bob asked.

"He wants me to write about the initiation of Shitfish and Cornbread."

"I think I missed that meeting," Bob said after a pause.

"I know," I responded, "but you were supposed to have sent Bobby's Rules of Order for ratification."

"I never sent them, did I?"

"No, you didn't," I said, slightly sarcastically.

"Did that surprise you?" he asked.

"No, Bob," I said softly. "I actually kind of expected it."

I sat at my desk and pushed aside the various work orders pending for that day. I thought back to the initiation of Shitfish and Cornbread. There were questions I could not answer, like why men haze each other. Why can't we simply accept someone for who they are, especially if we know them well? Why must they prove themselves when they already have in crucial ways? But then, the Society was not your typical fraternity. It was more like Animal House than the order of the Freemasons. Our initiations were more or less a joke and I got to smiling about it as I put the pen to the page.

Roger Shitfish was a Swamp Yankee, one of an ever-dwindling breed who invariably trace their lineage directly back to the Mayflower. Swamp Yankees are typically stubborn, tough, tenaciously independent, and slow to trust. They are survivors and throwbacks to an earlier age.

I met Roger nearly twenty years ago when I endeavored to learn to play the five-string banjo. All I knew was that when I heard banjo music, it reached something deep inside me. I felt it at the core of my being and it made the hair on my arms stand up.

Shitfish tying one on

I went to a music store in Providence and purchased a beginner banjo and inquired of the proprietor who might teach me to play it. He directed me, after some silent deliberation, to Roger, who lived in a nearby town. He cautioned me, "He's not your usual sort but he's the best damn banjo picker I've ever heard."

That night I called him. The flinty voice on the other end, mellowed by years of tobacco use, reminded me of my wife's grandfather who "commenced to do things." An old Yankee himself, he recalled taking the stagecoach from Swansicut to Providence in his youth. I explained to Roger that I had been given his name and that I wanted to learn to play the banjo.

"Why?" he asked, after a long pause.

I groped for words. I couldn't find any. After an awkward silence, we arranged to meet at his house the following Wednesday evening and we would talk. I hung up the phone realizing that he had agreed only to meet me, not to teach me.

I sat in the kitchen of the house he had built completely by himself. The wood stove hissed and crackled and after a half hour of stilted, guarded conversation, he arose from the chair and disappeared without excusing himself. He returned a few moments later with a large bottle of Yukon Jack and mismatched glasses. He lit a Parodi, filled our glasses, drained his in a swig, and settled back in a haze of smoke and winked at me.

I felt transported in time as I gazed across at the wiry man sitting across from me. His hair was starting to gray and his bushy sideburns reached far below his ears. A stubble of a mustache, perhaps only several days old, was forming on his lip. Age lines and the creases formed by time spent outdoors criss-crossed his face. It was his eyes, however, that stood out. They were not very large or odd-shaped – they were simply very bright, hinting at deep intelligence.

We talked long into the evening and although we came from distinctly different backgrounds, we sensed a common spirit in each other. Roger simply could not tolerate bullshit, nor could I. He could sense it in all its various disguises and smell it at a distance as keenly as a deer could smell a human upwind.

Roger agreed to teach me to play the banjo and in ensuing months I introduced him to Maypo. The three of us became fast friends, and he saw to it that Maypo and I became passable musicians. Over the course of the many Wednesday evenings spent at his house, fueled by Yukon Jack, we came to learn much about and from Shitfish. As he learned to trust us, he revealed more of himself. Not all at once, but more like the petals of a flower falling gradually away from the stem, leaving the iris vulnerable and exposed.

Shitfish had very little formal education, yet he had been employed as a machinist for most of his adult life. He had built black powder weapons from scratch, along with knives, miniature blacksmith shops, doll houses, and just about anything one could imagine requiring expert craftsmanship. He also was indeed the best damn banjo picker I ever heard. He had played the Grand Ol' Opry and his Bluegrass band was routinely booked year-round.

In addition to his mechanical ability and banjo prowess, Roger Shitfish was an avid hunter and fisherman. Over the years, Maypo, Lyle and I have spent many evenings fishing and swapping stories with Shitfish. In the aftermath of the one night gathering in the gravel bank, Maypo, Lyle, Buck and I began to yearn for a real Rendezvous. El Whippo was on sabbatical in the United Kingdom. Cosmos was working for a defense contractor on the west coast and Bobby had moved to Washington to work on his third marriage. None of us had ever met her, but Bob assured us that she gave great blowjobs.

"In fact," he said, by way of describing his third wife, "When she's suckin' on that thing, sometimes I'm afraid she could make all of me simply disappear into her mouth. God, I love it!" he said.

But I digress.

We were hoping to all come together for a real fishing trip in the coming summer. In the meantime, our ranks, in view of the absence of Whippo, Cosmos, and Bob, were temporarily depleted. We needed two things: more members and a winter dinner meeting.

Roger Shitfish and Kevin "Cornbread" Feeley were the obvious new recruits. My brother and I had known Kevin for years. Although he was a couple of years older, he and I had played on the same high school basketball team during my sophomore year. Though short of stature (he claims to be five-eight), Kevin was an excellent shooter. The problem he presented for me and the rest of his teammates was that he simply would not pass the ball. I recall one game in particular in which he took nineteen shots in the first half alone. He only made three of them, prompting an exasperated Coach Bennett to chide him at half-time.

Cornbread tying one on

"Goddammit, Feeley! I swear, son, if you could shoot from the damn locker room, you would."

Following college, Kevin simply couldn't find a job. All I had to offer him was a boring, low-level, unskilled job working third shift at Sullivan Sand and Gravel. From eleven p.m. to seven a.m., Kevin diligently oiled and lubricated heavy machinery that would work nearly sixteen hours straight the following day. Eventually, Kevin worked his way into the office, where he is employed to this day.

In addition to his jumpshot, Kevin possessed an uncanny and uninhibited sense of humor. There wasn't much that didn't strike him as funny. If a thought came into his head that tickled his funny bone, he was at a loss to prevent himself from expressing it. Bobby once aptly described him as a "funny little shit." When the two of them got together, they would play off each other like a seasoned comedy team. Eventually, their respective contagious laughter would leave both of them incapacitated and the rest of us holding our sides. As a result, Kevin was, primarily for this reason, a natural for the Big Blue Society.

We arranged to meet at Maypo's cottage on a Friday night in early March. Constance was out of town visiting her sister and Maypo thought that fact alone was worthy of celebration. He made a large pot of chili and invited me, Lyle, Whippo, Buck, Kevin and Roger Shitfish. The agenda for the evening would be to drink beer, eat chili, smoke a bone, ratify Bobby's Rules of Order and initiate the new members of the Society.

Nobody knew what the initiation should be. Bobby wouldn't be there, so the threat of being popped from behind would be an idle one. Kevin, Buck and I discussed it at work and Kevin expressed reservations about having to be initiated.

"Look," he said," I've known you guys for most of my life. We work together, for Chrissakes. Why do I have to be initiated into anything?"

"But Cornbread, we were planning on flying the Bob-man in from Washington to pop you from behind," I said in response.

"That's what I'm afraid of," he said. "I might like it."

We chuckled and agreed to suspend the initiation for little Cornbread, but we were still left with the problem of how to initiate

Shitfish. During our discussion, I had observed Buck and Kevin exchanging glances, prompting me to ask what they knew that I didn't.

"Why don't you leave Shitfish's initiation up to us?" Buck stated. "Kevin and I think we have it under control."

That night when I arrived at Maypo's, the smell of chili greeted me in the driveway. Upon entering, I encountered Lyle sitting at the kitchen table, nursing a Corona. We exchanged greetings in the form of the Big Blue handshake and I inquired about the fresh scab and the puffiness on his upper lip. Lyle averted my gaze, but Maypo emerged in the doorway, holding the twisted remnants of a saxophone and was eager to explain Lyle's most recent affliction.

"This is the culprit," he declared, holding forth the damaged instrument.

I noticed that the mouthpiece was broken in half and the other end was crumpled in upon itself like a deflated football. Lyle sucked on the Corona and reminded me of a pet caught in the act of raiding his master's trashcan. Maypo explained that several nights earlier in that same house, a severely incapacitated Lyle, inspired by John Coltrane, had attempted to play along on his recently purchased sax. The sounds that he made couldn't actually be called musical, but he was not to be deterred. Despite several complaints from neighbors, Lyle had paraded around Maypo's house like some crazed, trumpeting elephant. Eventually, Maypo explained, everything caught up with Lyle at once. Fatigue, alcohol, pot and perhaps his own aversion to the pitiful sounds he was making combined.

Maypo said, "One second he was standing there and the next he fell like a house of cards. He landed on the horn with the thing still in his mouth."

I glanced at Lyle. He looked away and sucked deeply on his beer.

"Sounds like more charges coming up," I said.

"Story of my life," Lyle said, staring out the window.

A short while later, we were joined by Whippo, Buck, Kevin

and Shitfish. We popped some beers and indulged in Maypo's chili, which was on the spicy side. He remarked that, "Constance won't eat it because it makes her tongue go numb."

"Why should that bother you?" Lyle asked.

"Fuck you, Lyle." Maypo responded.

Maypo revealed the fact that Bobby, true to form, had not sent along his Rules of Order for ratification. "All is not lost, however," he continued, "because I have a movie of the smelting trip and we do have ol' Roger's initiation to deal with."

The "Smelting Trip" Maypo was referring to had occurred several months earlier in the dead of winter. At the request of Shitfish, six of us piled into one of the Sullivan Company vans. The delivery van had no seats other than for a driver and a passenger, but that was not a problem. We took a couple of old couches from the yard foreman's office and set them in the back. We filled a trashcan with ice and beer and set off.

Maypo drove thirteen hours that day. We got lost twice on Shit-fish's directions. We finally arrived at our destination, a frozen bay on the coast of Maine. I recall the setting resembling a shantytown with rows of small huts spread across the frozen surface. We spent several hours huddled together in one of those small, cramped huts, staring collectively at a hole in the ice. On two occasions, when the tide came in and when the tide went out, we caught fish. They were about the size of my thumb. Shitfish cooked them, bones and all, with potatoes, peppers and eggs. We stood outside our shanty, freezing our asses off and ate every bite. Then Maypo drove 6 hours home.

We retreated to Maypo's den and he rolled the film. There was a shot of all of us standing outside the van at first light. Buck had his middle finger extended. There was a shot of all of us crammed into the van. The photographer must have been in the rear of the vehicle. There was a shot of a smiling Lyle with his twinkling blue eyes. There was suddenly a shot of a big set of naked breasts followed by a shot of a smiling Lyle. There was a shot of me holding a single smelt dangling from a tiny hook. There was a shot of a penis resting comfortably inside a woman's mouth, followed by the previous shot of a smiling Lyle. Maypo had edited the film and inserted pornographic scenes between the repetitive frame of Lyle's happy face.

Following the film, we settled with fresh beers onto the couches in the den. Buck, our Grand Scrotum, presided. He stood in the middle of the room and began by saying, "Gentlemen, we are gathered here this evening...." and then he paused and looked around the room like an actor in search of a cue.

"Why the fuck are we gathered here this evening?" he continued, starting to laugh.

"Initiation," Kevin prompted.

"Oh, yeah." Buck said. "We are gathered here to initiate Roger Shitfish and Kevin "Cornbread" Feeley."

"Here, here!" Whippo cheered, confident in his role as a full-fledged member.

I glanced at Roger, who was looking at Kevin. Roger wore a concerned look in contrast to Kevin, who appeared simply delighted.

"How do I get myself into these situations?" Shitfish deadpanned in typical Yankee understatement.

Buck continued his rambling, drunken monologue in which he eventually got around to describing what the initiation would be.

"It is imperative that all current Big Blue members and those hoping to become members rise at this time and show us your dicks."

At this moment, I was beginning to think that Buck had lost his few remaining senses. Meanwhile, however, Kevin slowly stood and I watched in amazement as his hand went to his zipper. I glanced at Shitfish who had frozen with his beer poised on his bottom lip and a look that registered both fear and confusion.

Kevin, meanwhile, had unzipped his fly and was reaching inside. When his hand emerged, the biggest prick I had ever seen in my life came with it. It was damn near as big around as a beer bottle and it hung nearly to his knee. He held onto it with both hands as if it might get loose in the room. Now, that whole scene was unsettling enough, but to compound matters was the fact that the prick in question was as black as freshly laid asphalt.

Apparently, Buck and Kevin had crafted the king penis from caulking compound used to plug the air space around the windows of one of the drafty garages at Sullivan Gravel. To this day, Roger Shitfish says, "I have to admit, I thought at first that little fucker is really hung like a fuckin' bull. It took me a few seconds to figure it out."

"Didn't the fact that it was black kind of tip you off?" Maypo asked.

"Not if you've seen as much shit as I have in more than sixty years," Shitfish responded.

The true genius of humanity lies in its incompetence.

Stephen Pile

Green Island

THE NOT-TERRIBLY-GOOD CLUB of Great Britain believes that humans stand out in one area: failure. Under the direction of Stephen Pile, they compiled, "The Incomplete Book of Failures," a collection of stories, anecdotes, and facts that evidence their belief. They celebrate the likes of the Thomas Nuttall, an 19th century explorer who got lost so often his comrades had to light great fires at night to guide him back to camp. They revel in the tourist who deplaned in Los Angeles and thought he was in Rome... for 3 days. Incompetence in every arena - thieves who rob shuttered banks, animal rescues gone terribly wrong, misguided wars, empires lost - people doing what they do best: being inept. Given Buck's "leadership" of the Big Blue, I believe the Not-Terribly-Good Club would be impressed.

Buck promised to lead the Society forward, but in his role as the Grand Scrotum he didn't do a damn thing for 10 years. He had one job - to arrange a Rendezvous, and he made no move in that direction. We lodged our complaint, and Buck felt misunderstood.

"I knew it required someone to do a shitty job," he said, "I just didn't know if I was up to it."

Buck was more than up to it. His flawed leadership was a prime example of what the Big Blue was about. We were not a well-oiled machine. We were not a machine of any sort. We were a hapless bunch of guys who couldn't get it together to go on a fishing trip. If we left it up to Buck, we might never go on another.

Then a stroke of luck befell the Society when our high-flying brother Cosmos sold his med-tech company, quit the west coast and crashed like a meteor in a back room at Sullivan Sand and Gravel. He was 35, powerfully built, bushy red beard off-setting thinning blond hair. He had come home to chart the next chapter in his life and was drawing up plans for a sailing kayak that resembled a spaceship. We wanted to reconnect with our brother and could think of no better way than taking him on a full-fledged Rendezvous.

Sausage kicked into high gear and called the Bobman in Washington. He was recovering from a stomach operation in which surgeons replaced his shredded abdominal wall with Marlex (think window screen). The Bobman was in no shape to go on Rendezvous no matter how good the Sausage's plan, and the Sausage's plan was great. He took stock of our scouting report on Saranac Lake, chartered a plane and handed out tickets to Buck, Shitfish, and Cosmos. Lyle and Whippo were out. Lyle's wife was about to conjugate the greatest verb of all time, "birth," and Whippo was on sabbatical in England. I was sent as the advance party to secure Green Island, pick up the men at the Saranac airport, and guide them to the site. The Big Blue was on the move again.

∾

I left early on a Friday morning and got behind the wheel of Sausage's Jeep Cherokee that was preloaded with coolers and gear. I drove the 6 hours to Hidden Bay Marina on Lower Saranac Lake and rented a canoe. I knew the best campsites would be in demand and set out to claim Green Island. There were no reservations in those days, and I hoped it would be free.

I paddled with purpose, the same way I drove, and Green Island came into view at high noon. No boat was landed on the flat rock, no tent was pitched cliffside, no smoke rose through the trees. I cracked my first beer of the day and toasted the mountains and sky. My brothers were coming to the most stunning place I had ever been and we had 5 days with nothing to do but kick back, relax and —

A red canoe rounded the far tip of the Green Island with a couple on board. Their canoe was loaded with gear and they were looking for a campsite. I put the beer down and turned j-strokes leaving vortexes behind that sucked air. I wished Lyle was in the bow pulling hard with his long arms. I made a beeline for the rock, but the red canoe landed first and I went off in my head.

That's our fucking island! Lyle and I scouted it weeks, months, years ago! You can't just pull up and lay claim. You can't walk up the path, check out the picnic table, look off the cliff. You can't discuss the pros and cons… the hill's steep, the picnic table's wobbly, the outhouse disgusting. You don't know fucking shit! That's Big Blue Island!!!

Like I said, I went off.

The guy was wearing a French cut bathing suit and the girl was braless under a tank top. They saw me coming in hot and looked confused. They were there first, right? To cement their position, the guy took a Styrofoam cooler out of their canoe and set it down.

I rode up high and hard on the rock, grabbed my pack and started up the path. No word of greeting, no eye contact, I was on a mission. A cooler was nothing. Hell, they could be on a picnic. A tent was a statement, a declaration. I pitched mine in record time. Green Island was ours!

I returned to the canoe for the first of my 3 coolers and found the couple in heated debate. They spoke French, which made them seem out of a foreign film in which the couples fight, fuck, and repeat. The guy was pissed I was an uncouth American. The girl was annoyed he was such a pussy. I hauled a heavy cooler like it weighed nothing and smiled as I passed.

The smile did it. The guy started pitching their tent 15 feet up the path. The girl puzzled poles while he tried to stake a corner into solid ledge. I galumphed past, grabbed another cooler, and paused to enjoy their struggle.

A dome tent looks all wrong before it comes right. You bend a pole to the breaking point and the nylon threatens to split. The crossmember sticks out like a dislocated bone while you try to stab the opposing corner. Before the tent pops into being, it looks like a crashed weather balloon. Theirs was at that point. I feigned empathy. The girl huffed at me. I nodded and I moved on.

Their tent was up when I passed with the final cooler. A mess, but upright. I considered it, and them, and said, "It's ok if you stay the night, but you'll want to break camp in the morning. My brothers are coming."

"How many?" the girl asked, like she could handle a few.

"Six," I said, a solid number.

They were fighting when I set the cooler by the picnic table. Poles hit the ground in an angry clatter, nylon hissed as it was balled into a jumble. There were mutters, curses, and objects flung into a canoe. Then all went still.

I took a beer cliffside for a look-see. They paddled by a safe distance from shore. I toasted them with my beer, and the guy flipped me off. Fair enough. I stole the site out from under them. The girl swore under her breath. Got it, a spirited gal. I was sure they were going to fuck that night.

Alone with my thoughts and a baked potato, I focused on Cosmos. He had taken a different path than his brothers, one that gained him advanced degrees, patents, and a home in the Palisades. He always did things his own unique way which fueled the inventor in him. When Cosmos looked at a problem, he thought so far outside the box he disputed there was ever a box. A strident individualist, I wondered how he would fit in with the Society.

Roger Shitfish was another question mark. It's one thing to pick banjo in a smokey parlor or share a meal, quite another to camp together for days on an island. You share everything… boats, food, booze, space, even the shitter. You get to know a person well, too well sometimes. Roger had asked about Buck and Cosmos, and while we could vouch for Buck, our reference on Cosmos was 15 years old. Personality conflicts could threaten a trip like with Big Tom and Van. I polished off my potato and tossed the skin in the fire. I hoped everyone would get along.

I woke the next morning and wished I had Lyle's watch. I didn't know what time it was and the guys would hit the airport at 11. I ate a granola bar on the way to Hidden Bay and arrived at 10, just enough time to meet the guys if I didn't get lost, which I did. The Blues were waiting with their gear, toked up and crackling with excitement. We piled into the Cherokee and were off.

I hadn't noticed how crappy Hidden Bay Marina was until I saw it through my brothers' eyes. Everything was hanging on for dear life, especially the owner. Tubercles crisscrossed his face like a roadmap of every night he got shitfaced in his cabin. He rented us beat-up canoes and seemed to resent our brimming good spirits. Loading the canoes, he asked, "How long you going out for, a year?"

Buck knew the crack was coming, but there it was, and he wanted to tell the guy to fuck off. Instead, he nodded at him for a long time, taking in the full measure of the man. The owner left us alone after that.

Hidden Bay bore little resemblance to the pristine lake that Lyle and I had described. Pecky cabins lined the shore and rainbows of engine oil undulated by the dock. You couldn't see the lake until you broke out of the bay, but then it appeared in all its glory: distant shores, beckoning islands, weathered peaks cradling the lake. It was a lot to behold.

I rode with Buck who reveled in the beauty and freedom. He kept resting his paddle to take in the sights: sheer cliff dropping 100 hundred feet into the water, natural beach of gleaming white sand, shorelines dotted with boulders and crowded with Arborvitae revealing the snow depths with their bare bottoms.

"They look like ladies lifting their skirts," Buck said.

He was poetic like that.

Lower Saranac Lake

Cosmos slipped out of his canoe and swam alongside us, buck naked. Sausage once mused about a Big Blue tattoo that would catch a coroner's eye: a pair of blue lips inked on our butts. Cosmos would have done it proud. His attitude was kiss my ass.

Everyone camps in their own style. Shitfish was a throwback

to the days when guys set off in the woods with little more than a hatchet and a bedroll. His tent was an oilskin tarp propped up with a stick. A woolen blanket was his sleeping bag, folded like a soft tortilla. His mess kit was a blackened skillet he fried worms in one night when the fish didn't bite. He said they were, "Crunchy."

In marked contrast, the Sullivan brothers were incredibly well outfitted. Sausage was an Eddie Bauer fanatic and had the best of everything. He looked like Gadabout Gaddis on safari in Africa. Buck was more modest by nature, but he had splurged on an igloo tent that took an hour to set up. I was devoted to my Eureka Alpine tent that was taut and self-supporting. Cosmos had a geodesic dome tent and a bag of tricks. He pulled out gizmos none of us had seen before, all super light and high tech: single burner cook stove/heater, L.E.D lantern, power coffee grinder. A self-admitted java snob, Cosmos couldn't stand the stuff that came out of a can, never mind the instant variety. His Kenyan blend was flight fuel.

Cosmos, Shitfish, Maypo, Buck, Sausage

Shitfish was not impressed. He thought the world was going to hell in a basket and the day would come when we'd have to survive on woodsman skills. He took it upon himself to teach us and set a dead fall trap by the picnic table. He carved a "trigger switch," propped it under a heavy stone, and baited it with pepperoni. Behind his back, Cosmos ate the pepperoni. It was the first sign of trouble between them.

Sausage dropped a Red Devil off the ledge and vertical jigged. Moments later, he hooked into a Northern Pike and we all gathered round. The first fish is always big because it suggests that we'll all be catching them soon. Sausage hauled the pike up the 25-foot wall and landed it on the granite flat. It was a thrilling start to a great week of fishing.

Buck broke out the horseshoes and called for a game. It was hard to find a level run between trees and there were no pits. We pounded posts and started playing Extreme Horseshoes. Our father taught us how to pitch and he threw a precise turn that brought the shoe in open to the post. He boasted fifty percent ringers in his heyday, a feat we never matched.

Buck's shoe was like our dad's, consistent and often deadly. Mine rotated in the wrong direction and tended to sail over the stake. Cosmos experimented with multiple rotations and Sausage's shoe incorporated a curious side flip influenced by body english. We tossed a few to warm-up and Shitfish joined in. He was skilled with real horseshoes, the kind with nails, but couldn't reach the pit with the tournament variety.

"Have you ever actually thrown a ringer?" Cosmos asked.

Shitfish muttered something and retreated to the Gentleman's Bar. He surveyed the offerings and took up an unassuming bottle of clear liquid Sausage brought. He gave it a whiff and recoiled.

"What is that?!"

"Grappa," Sausage said. "Italian moonshine."

Moonshine appealed to Shitfish so he took a deep pull. His eyebrows knit together and steam just about came out his ears.

"S-mooth," he said, thumping his chest to restart his heart.

Shitfish corralled the bottle, took up a position on a boulder by the pits and installed himself as the Grappa Judge. His judgment would be called upon to settle disputes which seemed fitting because after a few hits of Grappa, Shitfish couldn't judge a damn thing.

From the dawn of Sullivan family sports, Sausage and Buck squared off against Cosmos and me. They kicked our asses as kids, but it was time to settle the score. Riding the Cosmos's hot hand we blazed out to a lead and won the first game 21-9.

The pits were starting to take shape and Buck's shoe came around. He dropped in for point after point and Sausage threw a floppy ringer to win the second game 21-16. It was on to the rubber match.

Sausage is a wily cuss. He noticed that Cosmos unhinged after a couple tokes, so he rolled a babaloo. A babaloo is a joint with a fat, round center. When you get to it, the tokes are intense. Cosmos got to it and couldn't find the pits, never mind the post. Somehow, we hung in and the game was tied when Shitfish was hailed for a judgment call. He ruled in our favor and we took the lead, 21-20.

I was pitching against Buck and came through with double ringers, rare when the pits have rocks and roots that can kick a good shoe away. Cosmos started celebrating, but I focused on Buck. I had seen him rise to athletic challenges before. He let fly, and *clang, clang*. Not only did he throw double ringers, but he knocked one of mine off to win - the most clutch horseshoes ever pitched in Big Blue history.

Smoke wafted from the fire carrying with it the sweet aroma of pineapple. Sausage checked on the traditional ham wrapped in aluminum foil while Shitfish stabbed a potato from the coals. Buck cleared a place for himself at the table while Cosmos crowded it with salsa, refried beans, jalapeno peppers, chopped tomatoes, and grated cheese. He was making tacos for dinner, never one to settle for standard fare.

"This sucker's done," Sausage concluded, plopping the ham on the table. He cut long slabs off the bone and forked them onto our plates.

"That smells some good," Shitfish said.

We ate in relative silence, chewing sounds mixing with the wind in the trees. It had been a full day and appetites were big as they always are in the woods. Sausage filled Dixie cups with expensive wine chosen to compliment the ham. Buck ate slowly, savoring every bite. Shitfish chewed on the good side of his mouth and praised the tender ham. Cosmos ate standing up, inhaling his tacos and making strange sounds that I took to be satisfaction.

After dinner, we sat around the fire with cigars and passed the bottle of Yukon Jack, a 100 proof Canadian Whisky. The label said it was "born of hoary nights" and it did have a warming effect.

"I had a couple beauties on today," Shitfish said, "but they got away."

"Again?" I asked, in a kindly tone.

Shitfish got his Society name while hornpouting at the Attleboro Reservoir. The pout didn't bite until after dark, but Roger couldn't resist throwing a line out early. The result was what he called, "shit-fish," bluegills and perch. He complained while catching them, but the fact was he liked the action. The nickname stuck and belied Roger's solid fishing skills.

"Shitfish, let me ask you something," Sausage began.

Cosmos interrupted, "Have you ever actually caught a fish?"

Cosmos thought it was the funniest dig in the world. He reeled off into the woods and turned giddy circles through the trees. Shitfish raised his cup and took a sip, his eyes on Cosmos's backside.

In the morning, I found Shitfish alone at the picnic table while the others were out fishing. He was whittling a stick into a pile of slivers.

"I don't know how to take your brother," he said.

"I don't know how to take him myself sometimes."

Shitfish sucked at a gap between his teeth and looked out over the water. "I hope it doesn't come to blows."

Later that day, I talked to Cosmos. I asked him to ease up on Shitfish. Busting balls assumes a level of trust which wasn't in place. Cosmos looked at me with two sets of eyes. One measured my request, the other said that no one tells him what to do.

"He thinks you don't respect him," I said.

"I don't," Cosmos replied.

I didn't know what to say. I didn't know if he was busting my balls or if he had a genuine disregard for our friend. I walked to the outhouse and took a thoughtful crap. Through a crack in the door, I saw Cosmos pluck pepperoni from a trap and chaw it down. I figured it might come to blows.

Cocktail hour rolled around and Shitfish broke out his banjo. He tuned it up with his ear cocked to the side like a hunting dog hearing his master's call. He had come a long way from his first banjo, the one he made from a snare drum and a 2 x 4. Now he wrung the neck of a pre-war Gibson that had seen the countless festivals and the Grand Ol' Oprey stage. Shitfish played so bright and per-flickity that the woods seemed to hush and listen. Sausage picked up a couple of spoons and rattled along. I threw in hollers when the music carried me away. Buck, who didn't dance because hockey players don't, tapped his foot under table. Cosmos sat there, mesmerized by the rolls and breakdowns until Shitfish closed out with a trance-binding run.

"How do you do that?" Cosmos asked.

Shitfish smiled. No explanation could suffice. Bluegrass banjo was a perfection all its own.

Cosmos and Shitfish became friends that night. They talked about science and UFOs. Shitfish let Cosmos in on a closely guarded secret: he was working on a "dynamo," a source of unlimited energy. Sausage and I knew about the highly classified project. Shitfish took us into his shed one night and showed us a flywheel with spinning magnets. He was out to harness centrifugal force. Shitfish ran the theory by Cosmos who asked questions and seemed impressed. I was surprised he didn't punch holes in the theory.

When Shitfish wandered off to take a piss, I asked Cosmos if the dynamo could work.

"It's perpetual motion. Thermodynamics says no."

"But you didn't say that."

"I don't have to. He'll find out for himself."

I thought it was kind of Cosmos not to dash Shitfish's hopes. Who knew, maybe the dynamo would work. Maybe a swamp Yankee would solve the puzzle and provide unlimited energy for the world. That was the dream. Why destroy it?

"Buck," Sausage said in a serious tone, "it's time you call this meeting to order."

"I was afraid of that," Buck said, a half-eaten package of vanilla wafers in hand.

"You're up on charges, Buck," Sausage said. "Read 'em off, Maypo."

Cosmos pumped the lantern and I opened my notebook to the charges Bobby and I drew up. Ten years had passed since Buck was elected and he was headed for the Hall of Shame.

Gathering steam with every line, I read:

"Whereas Buck has done squat for the Society and, in so much, has shown contempt for the Big Blue mission and purpose; whereas Buck has considered himself a sacrificial lamb, and did not arrange a Rendezvous; whereas Buck promised to lead the Society forward, but led us astray, I do hereby motion for his removal from office."

"I second that," Shitfish said.

Buck stuck a cookie in his mouth and took in his accusers. He admitted that he had been deficient in his duties. He said he never wanted to be the president in the first place.

"I took office to save face and get a little head. My hands have been tied, but that didn't stop me from jerking off. My record is what it is. So fuck you."

Buck left with a presidential salute. He hung his dick out his shorts and Sausage reminded him that it was the sole right and privilege of office. Buck didn't care. He flashed it again. The salute was his legacy.

The fishing was great all week; one will suffice. Cosmos was fighting a pike that dragged the canoe after it, and Buck tried to bare-hand it out of the water because they had no net. He hauled it over the side of the canoe and the fish slipped his grip. It hit the gunnel crosswise and fell into the canoe, not out. Things don't usually happen like that, but they did on this trip.

On the morning of the last day, Sausage scrambled eggs. Cosmos offered me the last of the grappa and I shuddered at the thought, still tasting it from the night before. Sausage emptied the bottle into the skillet.

"Grappa eggs," he said.

Cosmos style

Buck needed a semblance of order to eat and cleared a place at the cluttered picnic table. Cosmos, on the other hand, stood. Most of the stuff on the table was his. Taco shells wallowed in rainwater along with sides of refried beans, jalapeno relish, Goldschlager, and coffee grounds. Cosmos didn't clean up after himself on Rendezvous. I think it conflicted with his sense of Big Blue freedom.

Shitfish made a spot for himself on the bench, and I sat on my cooler, not wanting to deal with the table. Buck went to his cooler for ketchup and stood back. The mayo jar floated in meltwater that looked like urine. I ventured it was caused by a mustard leak, but Buck didn't want to chance it. He had his eggs plain.

The conversation turned to the flight home, and Buck was anxious about flying in small planes - too many mishaps, too many crashes. Shitfish, to his credit, was earning his pilot's license. Buck asked him if he could handle the plane in case of an emergency.

"Say the pilot has a heart attack, could you land us safely?"

"Sure," Shitfish said, a fleck of egg shooting out between his teeth.

We watched that bit of egg fly through the air, deflect off the bench and land on a rock.

"What if the engines cut out and we were going down?" Buck asked. "No airport, just woods. What would you do?"

Shitfish took a swig of coffee from his battered metal cup, playing it out in his mind. Cessna 172, five men, overloaded with gear, fighting to keep the nose up.

"In that case, I'd mush 'er into the trees."

Mush didn't sound like the kind of thing you want to do with plane. Shitfish flew his hand through the air.

"I'd come in soft over the trees and settle 'er into the tops."

Buck pushed his plate away, appetite gone. An unspoken concern was we'd go on one of these trips and not return. Someone would have an accident, or die even. It would be hard to defend the mission of the Blues after that, but we always got home safe... for the most part.

"Sure was different without the Bobman," Sausage said as we loaded the canoes.

"Not half as wild," Buck agreed.

"Lyle would have added something," I said.

"Yeah, the lip," Sausage quipped.

We shoved off, Cosmos and Shitfish in one canoe, Sausage and Buck in another, and I paddled the barge full of black trash bags. For all we ate, burned and drank, the loaves and fishes of garbage happened on every trip. Approaching Hidden Bay, I looked back at the welcoming arms of Lower Saranac and vowed to return with the Society in full force.

Bob

Life is too important to talk seriously about.

OSCAR WILDE

BOBBY'S RULES OF ORDER

I WAS SITTING IN my kitchen, working out the lead to "Cripple Creek," when Bob appeared at my door. He had lost a few pounds since I saw him last, but he was still the same behemoth it was hard to get your arms around. He lifted me off the ground in a bear hug.

"How's it hanging, Maypo?"

His standard greeting.

Bob was visiting from Washington where he wrote high-powered briefs for the Disabled American Veterans. He also acted as an attorney, representing vets in court over injuries and settlements. Not bad for a guy with a G.E.D. He had recently argued the case of a dick-damaged vet who sought fair compensation for his mangled meat. The settlement group maintained that the vet's member still functioned and did not qualify for disability. Bob thought they were missing the point on aesthetic grounds. He had a photo of the member in question blown up poster size and set it before the court.

"This soldier lost his fireman's cap," Bob said. "Who would want to fuck that?"

The case was settled with full compensation.

I popped a couple beers and Bob pulled a legal pad out of his travel bag. In his flowery hand, he had written his version of Robert's Rules of Order for the Big Blue Society. I present them to you now unedited and unabridged.

BOBBY'S RULES OF ORDER

Statement of Purpose

The Big Blue Society is a journey with no destination in sight. It is an asylum without walls. Our singular chartered purpose is to ensure that at least some of the lines etched in the faces of time are the result of laughter.

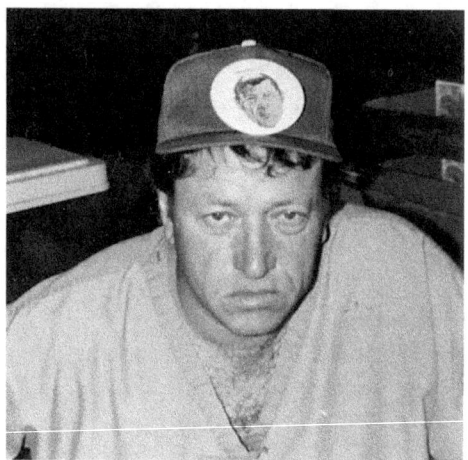

The Bobman

Goals of the Society

The Society provides for Rendezvous where men will be men. With no special emphasis, we promote the following: fishing, drinking, farting, grunting, merriment and mayhem.

Big Blue Motto - Go For It.

Society Slogan – Deny Everything.

ARTICLES OF INCORPORATION

Article 1 - Membership

Any male is eligible for membership upon unanimous vote of the Society. All Society decisions are final. No individual shall be denied membership due to race, creed, national origin, age, or penis size.

Section 1: Termination

A unanimous vote is required to terminate members.

Article 2 - Meetings

The Grand Scrotum shall call meetings and notice shall be given to all members.

Section 1: Attendance

Though attendance is not mandatory at meetings, members may be charged with contempt for Society spirit which may lead to termination.

Section 2: Quorum

Six or more members constitutes a quorum and may vote on matters that effect other members of the Society.

Article 3 - Fiscal Policies

Section 1: Budget

The Society shall operate under a budget set forth by the official Deuschbaggin for the purchase of inebriates, stimulants, food supplies, and marital aids (when indicated).

Section 2: Fund Management

All monies received by the Deuschbaggin shall be placed in the Big Blue piggy bank and must be spent on matters set forth under Society Goals.

Article 4 - Rendezvous Rules

Rule 1: Big Blue Salute

The highest tribute that may be paid to any member of the Society is the Big Blue Salute. The official Salute is a full moon. The only exception will be from those members who suffer cheek deformity.

Rule 2: Mounting

Mounting may not take place during an official salute due to the disadvantage of the saluting member.

Rule 3: Elections

Elections, which may or may not take place on Rendezvous, are governed by majority rule.

Rule 4: Voting Privileges

Unconscious members enjoy full voting privileges. However, a grunt or groan may only be deciphered by the Grand Scrotum.

Rule 5: Nominations

Any member in good standing (not necessarily standing) may nominate an individual for Big Blue Offices. However, a second is required and may only be made by a member with a blood alcohol count of .235 or greater.

Rule 6: Deserting Members

At the close of Rendezvous business, members may return to their permanent abodes. Should a member choose not to return, the Society is sworn to secrecy as to the whereabouts of the deserting member.

Rule 7: Big Blue Farts

Fracturing of the atmosphere should not exceed the decibel level of a busy New York City street corner at the peak of rush hour.

Rule 8: Pest Control

A resolution having been adopted, the Grand Scrotum shall appoint a committee of one for Pest Control. Whenever possible, this appointment should be directed to the last man standing who is, by virtue of his staying power, the best man for the job. Under no circumstances, should Lyle be appointed to this position since he has been known to invade other members beer coolers after lights out.

Rule 9: Fish Mounting

Blue members may mount their respective catches, however they should seek permission from fellow anglers to mount a fish caught by another member. Under no circumstance, should a Blue use this as an excuse to mount a fellow Blue. Mounting is restricted to the catch of the day.

Rule 10: Lower Lip Protrusion

Protrusions in excess of 5 centimeters should be brought to the attention of the Scribbling Asshole and noted. Drool associated with this affliction will serve to satisfy the Blood Alcohol level required in Rule 5.

Rule 11: Contraband

The Society recognizes no such fucking thing.

Rule 12: Campfires

The gathering of firewood is the responsibility of the entire Society. This should be accomplished as close to arrival as possible. It should be noted that the outhouse, picnic tables, or any permanent structure, do not satisfy the definition of usable firewood except in case of extreme emergency.

Rule 14: Firewood Emergencies

On the last day of Rendezvous, or in the event of an overdose, a firewood emergency may be declared. In the event of such emergency, the outhouse should not be ignited while occupied by a Society member.

*The one serious conviction that a man should have
is that nothing is to be taken too seriously.*

Samuel Butler

ÉTOUFFÉE

In the Winter of 1990, Sausage had what I took to be a quiet nervous breakdown. Some questioned his relentless pursuit of excellence. Others said that he carried the world on his shoulders. I found him in his office at Sullivan Gravel staring out the window at the pit. His desk was piled high with interoffice memos, letters from the charitable foundations, lyrics to bluegrass songs he had abandoned, and employee compensation guidelines he was drafting. I opened a map of Lower Saranac Lake, blanketed his desk, and pointed to Site #45.

"It has a lean-to, plenty of space for tents, and good pike fishing in the shallows."

Sausage sighed as he did so often that year and sat down. He had given up playing the banjo and no longer joined me for picking sessions in Shitfish's kitchen. I did not understand how he could stop playing the instrument that brought him so much joy, but I knew not to push him. Sausage was a complex guy with deep rivers of feeling running beneath his stoic exterior. He said he didn't have the heart for the banjo anymore, and I was afraid it extended to the Big Blue.

"I don't think I'll go this year," he said. "My stomach's been out."

Sausage had recently gone on Prozac and was jittery. The doctor told him that the side effects would subside, but Sausage was crawling inside his skin. I didn't know about depression at that point and thought a Big Blue trip would settle his nerves.

"Bobby's coming," I said. "Lyle too. It's a full-blown Rendezvous."

"Really? You got the Bob man?"

"Flying in on the 25th. He'll crash at my place and then we'll head up. It's all set."

"What about Whippo?"

"He's got summer courses to teach."

"Buck and Cosmos?" Sausage asked.

"That depends on you. Are you coming?"

The Sausage

Sausage spiraled into himself, riding out an inner storm. Here was my oldest brother, the guy I looked up to in work, family, and sports, trembling. I wanted to help him, but I hadn't hit the black ice of mid-life yet. Sausage leaned back in his chair, laced his fingers behind his head for a moment, then hunched forward. He said he'd go. I think he didn't want to let us down.

We hit site #45 in the afternoon under heavy cloud cover, Sausage, Buck, and Bobby in one rented aluminum motorboat and Cosmos, Lyle, and I in another. We trailed a canoe behind as a nod to tradition. We pitched our tents quickly, collected firewood, and strung a tarp over the picnic table. Buck accelerated the fire with a Dixie cup of gasoline and we threw steaks on as it started to rain. We tended them from the open face lean-to and fell into the well-rehearsed cocktail hour drill.

Site 45 Lean-to

Buck and Sausage were in the Scotch phase, savoring the peaty goodness. Bobby was into pirate rum, convinced that it mixed with everything from Coke to coffee. Cosmos nipped at what everyone else had brought and added a few bottles of his own. His mixology was as ranging as his mind. He preferred nips to full bottles and combined potions like a mad scientist. Lyle was into beer-only, lots of it. I was dedicated to gin and liked the way Sausage served it up in cone-shaped glasses. "Martinis are like breasts," he said. "One is not enough and three are too many." I was up for a quartet that night.

The rain pounded on the roof of the lean-to and Sausage and

Buck talked about how it could really suck if the weather didn't turn. Lyle and I joked about our wash-out on Eagle Island, but camping in the rain is no fun. We ate the steaks and followed them with one of Lyle's overly tight joints. It was a thing of beauty, but impossible to toke. Only Lyle, with his Hoover lungs and saxophone lips, could get it to burn. It inevitably ran the side and he daubed it with saliva. After a second toke, he passed it on, eyes closed, with an attitude that he never wanted to see it again. If you complained, Lyle took offense.

"You roll," he'd say.

I did and called the meeting to order. At some point, I had been elected Grand Scrotum to fill the void left by Buck. I did my duty and organized a Rendezvous. Now it was time to get down to business.

"You're up on charges, Lyle."

"What is it this time?" he asked.

"The lip," Buck said, dragging his bottom one into a pout.

Lyle shook his head. There was nothing he could do about the lip. It puffed up after a few beers and fell with successive rounds. By the end of the night, it hung like a deflated inner tube on his chin. If the lip was grounds for charges, so be it. Lyle was not about to abandon his beer.

"Point of order," Bobby interjected.

"Go for it, Bob," I said.

"It has to do with you, Maypo." Bob dropped his cig butt into a neglected can of Bud. "I wasn't here when you got elected, but there seems to be a problem. It has to do with the Presidential Salute."

"Here, here," Lyle said, happy to have the focus shift from him to me. He sucked down a beer and spit out Bob's butt.

"What the fuck, Bob?"

"Lyle, you've got four or five going. How do I know which one's good?"

Lyle found a good one and Bob continued.

"Now Maypo, you've done a fine job of getting us here, but

you can't be the Grand Scrotum unless you salute us. Do you have a problem with that?"

"N-no," I said.

The guys laughed. Bob was a stickler for rules, not that he followed any, but to keep others in line.

"I say you salute us before we go any further."

I am an average guy, but the air was cold that night and, as I drew the leg of my shorts aside, the elements took their toll. Buck pumped the lantern several times and held it up to me.

"I detect a strain," he said. "A definite strain."

"I'm sorry Maypo," Bobby said, "I've seen clits bigger than that."

"But…"

"But nothing. The Grand Scrotum you ain't. We don't even need a vote. You're back to Scribbling Asshole."

Everyone was rolling in laughter, and I should have been too, but I had fallen into a Big Blue death trap: taking myself too seriously. I resigned as the Scribbling Asshole and Lyle volunteered. The next morning, he made his first entry.

∽

Few places in the natural world inspire a contemplative lifestyle and even mystical experiences. Saranac Lake, located in the Adirondack Mountains, is such a place. The origins of serenity were born here.

The early summer sun, only an hour past dawn, compels one to shed external skins for essential ones. The lake is shrouded in a blue haze, the Loud Silence unbroken except for the occasional click of a bale, whir of a fishing line, and plop of lure entering the water.

Suddenly, the canoe from which Sausage and Bobby fished listed to starboard. Bobby discharged a fart of gargantuan proportions. This was not your basic fishing trip fart but one of such magnitude and duration as to startle nesting loons a full 300 yards across on the far shore. They immediately took flight. How bad was it? Its duration - 20 to 25 seconds. Its sound – ungodly. Its odor, words do not do justice.

Sausage released his vice grip from the side of the canoe, grabbed his paddle and began stroking furiously... to no avail. The pungent, invisible cloud had enveloped the entire area. With forced resignation, he retched a couple of times and lit into Bobby.

"That has to be the most disgusting fucking thing I've ever heard or smelled!" Sausage declared.

Bobby, though relieved, was somewhat astounded himself. "Sorry Saus, what can I say. N.B.F., Natural Body Function."

"Natural, my ass. That was direct from the animal kingdom."

Bobby had no comeback, so he changed the subject. "Hey Sausage, did we really impeach Maypo last night?"

"Sure did, Bob," said Sausage with a chuckle.

"Why did we do that anyway?" asked Bob, genuinely concerned.

"There's no 'why' in the Big Blue. Shit happens. Now we get to elect you. Here's the plan...."

Sausage talked in a hushed tone. I could not hear his words, but at the end, Bobby exclaimed, "That's brilliant, Saus."

This is a true and accurate account of the goings on. Recorded by Lyle, the Scribbling Asshole.

Clouds rolled in from the west and mired us in a cold front. The fishing turned off and the overall mood was flat, especially Sausage. He was not his joke-telling, ball-busting, rabble-rousing self. He seemed to be going through the motions, and white-knuckling it at that. I found him on the rocky peninsula looking at the sky and tried to rouse him with 20-year-old scotch.

"Come on, Sausage, have a hit."

Out of nowhere, Lyle appeared. "Leave him alone, Maypo, he's not feeling good."

Lyle dropped in beside Sausage. I thought he was going to lend an empathetic ear, but instead Lyle started talking about his own problems. His wife was not happy. She was always complaining about his job, his hours, and the grit under his fingernails. She was good with the kids, but when it came to him, she had no patience.

"Did she give you a hard time about coming here?" Sausage asked.

Lyle wagged his head and took a long pull on the bottle.

"You deserve better," Sausage said.

"I have a problem with the word 'deserve'," Lyle said. "Who deserves what?"

"You deserve respect, Lyle. I mean, I give you a truckload of shit, but you know how I feel."

Lyle passed me the scotch. He and his wife were not getting along, but neither were Connie and I. She was off at conferences to the point that she was never home and she liked it that way.

"What's the secret of a happy marriage? What's the key?" Lyle asked.

Sausage talked about commitment, communication, acceptance, and forgiveness. It sounded like the therapy he was in was having an effect, but then his words fell apart. In the end, he chalked it up one thing.

"Luck," he said.

Lyle and I drank to it.

On the evening of the third day, with no better weather in store, Sausage and Buck announced that they were leaving in the morning. I hadn't heard them discuss it, but Buck and Sausage seldom had formal discussions about anything. They knew each other's mind the way a point guard knows when his power forward is going to flash in the lane. Sausage looked to the sky, and Buck started to pack. Bobby was leaving too. Buck and Sausage were his ride.

Sausage had me heat up the Crawfish Etouffee he had shipped in on dry ice from Louisiana. It was a hearty gumbo of crawdads brought together in a creamy pink sauce. We used to catch the small, lobster-like crustaceans as kids and hook them up as bait. They flicked their tails madly and produced monster strikes. Here they were in my bowl, bright red whorls curled in upon themselves.

"I'm calling it an early night," Sausage said, tossing a nearly full plate into the fire. "It's Crash's birthday tomorrow, and I'd like to be there for it."

I started to say something, but Bobby cut me off.

"Goodnight, Saus."

Sausage, Buck, and Cosmos crashed. That left Bobby, Lyle, and me on the peninsula. A half-moon crept over the mountain and cast a shimmer on the water. Waves lapped against the aluminum boats and produced a hollow ring.

"It's over, Bob," I said.

"What's that?" he asked, lighting a cig.

"The Big Blue. It's our last Rendezvous."

Smoke came out Bob's nose and mouth as he spoke. "No fucking way. So long as one of us draws a breath, the Society lives on."

I thought he was wrong. I thought we'd never get together again. Camping had lost its allure. The woods, the fires, the jokes had run their course. They were our youth, this was our middle age.

Sausage and Buck were up before dawn. I heard them bagging garbage and loading their boat. They didn't wait for a cup of Cosmos' coffee. They were already gone.

I crawled out of my tent and saw them off. Bobby's thumb bit into the back of my hand. Buck pulled the chord on the motor. Sausage sat in the bow, staring into a thick fog. They throttled up and disappeared behind layer after layer of gauzy mist. By noon, I declared the Society dead.

Cosmos humored me. "It was born dead."

But I lived the eulogy that day. I drank for all the times we laughed, all the skinny dips in chilly water, all the mornings we crawled out of our tents and crashed in them at night. Cosmos went for a boat ride, basically to get away from me. Lyle said I was acting, "Lugubrious."

"What does that mean?"

"Morose to the point of ridiculous."

He was right, of course, but I had something in my craw.

We went for a paddle and found ourselves at Lonesome Bay where it all began. The bench had been cut from the sitting rock and carted away. The cabin was gone as well, barely an imprint of where it had been. There was no sign of the fire pit, and it felt like the past had been erased.

I found a clover leaf where our tent had been and opened my notebook to press it inside. On the page, Bob had written this:

What will we do when we get too old to go on these trips? We'll make a hypnagogic return to the days of the Big Blue.

"Hypnagogic?" Lyle asked. "What does that mean?"

I had to look it up. It's a drowsy period between wakefulness and sleep in which fantasies and hallucinations occur. When I asked Bob how he came up with it, he said, "I've done a ton of drugs over the years."

We went back to the campsite and Cosmos was still out. He returned at sunset having traveled upriver through a set of locks to Middle Saranac Lake. He said it was less developed with very few campsites. He thought we should go there for the next Rendezvous.

"Don't you get it," I said. "It's fucking over."

Cosmos reheated the Etouffee and handed me a bowl. I didn't taste it going down, but I did on the way up. As the moon rose over Ampersand Mountain, I stumbled into the woods and puked. Crawdads pulsed at my feet like hot little coals. I was wrong. The days of the Big Blue were not over. They had just begun.

April 17, 1991

Dear Brothers,

From the pen of the newly elected Scribbling Asshole, notations on the current state d' affairs of the Big Blue Society. A paradoxical quagmire of enigmatic pomp and circumstance is the fad these days. Blasphemous statements such as, "The Society is Dead!" permeate the air waves.

This monty will not be so easily dissuaded. To say the Society was nothing more than a Temporal Lobe Apparition is bullshit. Ephemeral? Blah!

Three members prematurely depart the Rendezvous and societal existentialism is bandied about like so many flopping shiners. Please. Weaker excuses have been offered for non-attendance or early bailouts without such negative ramifications.

The Big Blue Society will not go out with a whimper. It will last a blue moon. If it be a New Age of Apathy, hooray for lethargy. The sun rises where it don't shine. Faith is not an intellectual activity and I, for one, believe in second comings!

With highest regards,

Lyle

The Scribbling (in for the long run, or in with the long one) Asshole

Lyle in camp mode

Imagination was given to man to compensate him for what he is not; and a sense of humor was given to him to console him for what he is.

Mark Twain

Site 45

My ghost marriage ended in ghost divorce. Constance handled with the paperwork, and it was done. She got the bank account; I got the lake cottage. When Winter came and the lake froze, I skated at night, careful not to fall in. Lyle brought tremendous news in the Spring. We were going back to Saranac. Sausage had risen from depression and sent Bobby a plane ticket. Cosmos completed his kayak, Buck had used my divorce as an excuse, and Whippo was bringing his son, Seamus. New blood was flowing into the Society just in time. **Sausage takes the lead here**, singing about our triumphant return to Site 45.

On a sultry early June day a couple weeks ago, I was reviewing personnel files prior to a meeting with a management-consulting firm. My attention was periodically diverted by the hazy blue sky framing the swaying birch trees outside my office window.

The Memorial Day weekend had ushered in unusually warm

weather that I hoped would serve as a harbinger of a hot, dry summer. It was difficult to focus on work. My mind was drawn like a leaf on a gentle breeze, seduced by thoughts of the upcoming Big Blue Rendezvous. Soon, we would be returning to the Adirondacks and our favorite campsite, Number 45, on Lower Saranac Lake.

My reverie was interrupted by a phone call from Maypo. He explained that he and Lyle had just returned from a swim in the Reservoir. They had discussed the pending trip and bemoaned the fact that it was such a long ride to Saranac. Maypo suggested we consider Lake Kevin as an alternative. The ride would be considerably shorter and his research from the previous winter had indicated that there were a number of promising island sites on Lake Kevin.

I hung up and went in search of Buck. Maypo had promised to stop by momentarily with literature on Lake Kevin. I found Buck in the warehouse in conversation with Cosmos, who was affixing a Plexiglas bubble to the top of his spaceship boat. The project had languished since his return from the West coast while he got married, had kids, and became a Rolfer. Now he was focused on the flying boat in hopes of christening it at Saranac. I explained Maypo's reason for calling as we made our way outside the building. Within minutes, Maypo pulled into the parking lot and emerged from his silver Pathfinder. He was freshly shaven, attired in shorts, tee shirt and sandals. He wore the contented look of a man relaxed and, at the same time, invigorated by a long swim in a pristine body of fresh water.

Maypo presented the Lake Kevin alternative and, in the process, seemed to talk himself out of the idea. Cosmos studied the pictures of large, well-established "vacation" camps on the crowded lake and summed up our collective feelings.

"I think that would suck."

Maypo shrugged, rolled up the brochures and said, "Well, Saranac it is."

He walked to his vehicle and returned a few moments later

with a stack of pictures. He presented them to me and said, "These might help you when you write the chapter on that trip in 1991."

The four brothers huddled and passed the pictures. Occasionally, someone would hold up a shot and we would chuckle. Maypo withdrew a shot of Bobby in a pale green hospital smock. His face wasn't shown, but we knew it was Bob. His shirt was rolled up and his stomach hung over his shorts. His hands seemed to support the bloated beach ball of a belly. It was unmistakably Bob's because it was the size of a beer keg and it was perfectly bisected by an inch-wide indented scar that ran from his chest to his groin. On trips, Bob would periodically press the two halves together and ask if anybody wanted to "rub their Van Winkle in there."

Buck spotted a picture of the four of us taken almost ten years earlier. We were naked, standing on a rock ledge, framed by water and trees in the distance. Four similar yet distinct white asses highlighted by deep summer tans. We were in our mid to late thirties when the picture had been taken. Our bodies were sleek, toned and hard. Our faces turned to the camera displayed no age lines. Our buttocks were still firmly attached to our waists. They had yet to suggest the sag and shift that would portend the beginnings of old age.

"I wonder how different that same shot would look today?" Buck asked.

"I don't think I would want to see it," Cosmos responded as he tucked in his shirt over a paunch that had not appeared in the picture.

There was a group shot. Lyle with his arm around Bobby. Whippo, wearing a ridiculous pink Mom's Mabley type hat, leaned against Maypo. Cosmos pointed a pellet pistol at the camera. The only one smiling was Whippo's son Seamus. The rest of us looked like we had been belched from the belly of the Bowery. Unshaven, blood-shot eyes, greasy jeans and bandaged fingers from cuts and burns.

I returned to my office and reviewed the rest of the pictures. My thoughts were shrouded in pleasant memories reminiscent of the mist that blanketed Saranac before sunrise. I recalled that memorable trip in 1991. The previous year's trip to Saranac had not been pleasant for me. It was devoid of fun and the fellowship had been strained. I was in the midst of a clinical depression. I took no interest in work or sports. All things that had sustained me for forty years had lost their appeal. I wallowed in self-pity like an old, soggy baseball glove discarded in the outfield, left to the mercy of the elements.

My somber mood had affected my friends. The Rendezvous had assumed the air of a wake. Buck, Bobby and I had left a day earlier than intended. Maypo, Lyle and Cosmos had stayed behind. Maypo had imbibed that day to the point of illness. Lyle's lower lip had reportedly rested on his chin the entire day. Cosmos had left the campsite to explore and had returned only at nightfall. That evening around the campfire a somber, hung-over Maypo declared the Big Blue Society to be, "fucking dead." There had been no winter meetings that year. In April of 1991, however, Lyle had eloquently tendered an olive branch in the form of a letter to all members. The Society was not dead, he had opined. It was different. It was evolving. It was what it was, whatever that was. The affect had been to rally the troops.

There was a renewed anticipation in the mood of the Big Blues. My depression had ceased. I had emerged with a rejuvenated attitude toward life with the help of Prozac and effective counseling. My mood the previous year had served as an anchor around the collective necks of the Big Blues. Now I was energized. I found myself embracing Lyle's resurrection tour. Together, we would serve as catalysts for another trip. In mid-June of 1991, we set out once again for Site 45.

Bob, Maypo, and my brother Cosmos were in the advance party. They had left on Monday morning. On Tuesday morning at 5:00

AM I picked up Buck. I had been awake, tingling with anticipation most of the night. If he had wanted to leave at 3:00 AM, I would have been in his driveway.

The ride took about six hours. Only the last hour and a half, once through Albany, had been scenic. We pulled into Hidden Bay Marina shortly and purchased fishing licenses. We rented an aluminum boat equipped with a 9-horsepower motor, quickly loaded it with our gear, and set out across the still fog-shrouded lake for Site 45.

The aura of peace enveloped us as we cut serenely through the mist. In the distance, the tops of mountains were beginning to appear as the fog burned off. The glassy black water blanketed in pollen was surprisingly warm for a northern lake in mid-June. Buck piloted the boat by memory. Occasionally, he would pass a point and say, "I know where we are. We're O.K."

At one point, he cut the engine and we drifted silently. In the distance, we could hear an approaching engine. Suddenly, a small boat with a lone occupant emerged from the fog. Bobby's bulk perched at the tiller prevented the boat from achieving plane.

"Yo!" I shouted, just in time for Bobby to veer to his left, avoiding a collision. He coasted alongside and we exchanged greetings. His bloodshot eyes hinted at the previous night's revelry. "Where are you headed?" I asked.

"Need ice, man," he responded.

"Already?" Buck asked.

"Fucking Lyle," Bob moaned. "That fucker brought half the inventory in the Budweiser warehouse."

"How many coolers do you guys have?"

"One each," Buck told him.

"Well, that motherfucker brought three. One for food and two for beer and the fucking coolers are bigger than my refrigerator at home. So, he's outta ice in one already."

"Did Whippo and Seamus arrive yet?" I interrupted him.

"Not yet, but Maypo said they're due in sometime today."

Bob shoved off and Buck restarted the engine. Bob called to us as we drove off. I gestured for Buck to turn around. Bob was balancing uneasily on the middle seat in his boat. His pants were down around his ankles. He was bent at the waist and the middle finger in each hand was extended skyward in salute. His prodigious shrapnel-pocked ass wobbled to the rhythm of his swaying boat.

"I think I've seen enough," Buck said as he gunned the engine.

We arrived at Site 45 a short while later. Maypo and Cosmos greeted us, secured the boat, and helped us carry our coolers and gear to the center of the campsite. Nothing had apparently changed from the previous year. The sturdy, three-sided lean-to erected on concrete blocks dominated our surroundings. An old picnic table carved with worn graffiti stood adjacent to a small permanent fireplace a short distance from the shelter. Time hardened dirt paths interrupted by rocks and roots led from the main clearing. I spotted only three tents and asked who's missing. Maypo answered that he and Bob had something going and they were sleeping together. The truth was that Lyle was leery of Bob's snoring and had chosen a site about sixty yards from the rest of the tents. This was ironic in that Lyle and Bobby were infamously equal Major League snorers. We briefly discussed whether they should share a tent away from the rest of us.

Buck lugged his gear to an open spot and, amidst curses about having to sleep next to Bob's tent, began to unpack. When I picked up Buck that morning, I had stuffed two small duffel bags and a cooler into my Jeep. Buck had three-oversized hockey bags and a cooler. I had recalled almost dropping a nut while helping Buck load his stuff into my Jeep. I thought, "Wow, what the hell is this guy bringing? We're only going to be out here for a few days. Maybe he's managed to bring along a woman. But then, the Bob man would be jealous."

As Buck unpacked and began to erect his tent, the anonymous

weight in his duffels began to take shape. Lyle, Maypo and Cosmos were seasoned backpackers. Simple, high-quality, one-man tents sufficed for them. I needed a bit more space, but a two-man tent was adequate for me. But not for Buck. It appeared that Buck might have visited a camping show at the Providence Convention Center and absconded with the entire L. L. Bean exhibit. Buck's tent required more than simple assembly. In fact, it could have accommodated an assembly.

"What the fuck is that monstrosity?" Maypo inquired of a perspiring Buck.

"I need space," Buck answered.

Out came the air mattress that, once inflated with a portable bellows, was larger than the lean-to. Into the tent went the air mattress, a double sleeping bag, an oversized flashlight, and a stereo system as big as a cooler. Periodically, Buck would interrupt his rustling around inside the tent to flip us off.

Bobby returned with ice about the time that my tent was erected and I had popped my first beer.

"Speaking of Lyle," I asked, "Where is he?"

Cosmos pointed across an expanse of water and simply said, "Exhibit A."

My eyes followed his hand and it took me a few seconds to determine what I was seeing. There was a naked man lying on an inflatable raft, bobbing like a cork. Tethered to the mother ship was a support vessel. A second raft, a tad smaller, precariously supported a cooler that had been jury-rigged, assumably by the man on the raft. Lyle was on vacation, drifting where the currents would take him. This would be the case for the next three days. Little did we know at the time that in the space of those three days that this man would be unanimously elected our president, unanimously impeached, and render his impersonation of Julia Childs on a bad acid trip.

Whippo and Seamus

Later that afternoon, Whippo and Seamus arrived. Whippo was no longer a new member of the Society. He'd been initiated and, like a sophomore in college, he reveled in the role reversal of being an upperclassman. Gone was the tentative attitude and speculative hesitancy of the new member. Whippo was now flush with the inflated bravado of the seasoned veterans of the Society. He was anxious for his son Seamus to experience the smorgasbord of personalities and dubious pleasures unique to a Big Blue Rendezvous.

Seamus was a strapping, well-muscled, hundred and ninety pound twenty-year-old. He was a serious student and an equally serious boxer. He embarked from the boat, casually lugging a sixty-pound cooler, armed with a smile that would not waver over the course of the next few days. He'd been privy to talk about the Society from his high school days. He wasn't threatened or intimidated. He immediately embraced the camaraderie and easy banter of the other members. He eagerly awaited anything that would come his way. His enthusiasm was a natural fit for the Society. In appreciation, that night, around the campfire, Bobby nicknamed him, "Fresh Meat." Father and son exchanged high-five and clinked beer cans. They settled around the fire, flush with the heady fumes of accomplishment.

It was the custom of the Blues to bring copious amounts of alcoholic beverages on Rendezvous. In addition to the multi-colored beer coolers dotting the campsite, I watched as the picnic table became as fine a bar as existed in a gentleman's parlor. Single malt scotches, premium tequilas, and expensive grappe vied for space with the usual vodkas and gins. Each member contributed something to the communal bar and it remained open for business 24 hours a day.

We quickly made Site 45 our own. Whippo and Fresh Meat's tents joined the others. Horseshoe pits were dug. Towels were hung in trees or over an impromptu clothesline. I observed the interplay of colors and comments that afternoon as I sat at the picnic table. The afternoon light filtered through the spruce trees and reflected softly off the muted brown pine needle floor of our campsite. This would be our home for only a few days. It was now distinctly marked as a Big Blue Campsite in much the same way that a dog marks his territory with feces and urine. A contentment that settled over the place. The smell of the ever-present fire blended with the reflection of the sunlight though the smoke. It was accented by animated conversation interspersed with the clink of a horseshoe and pop of a beer. In previous times and days to come, Site 45 would host other campers. Married couples with young children, older couples and exuberant college kids. I'm sure that if Site 45 could express itself in language, it would have many stories to tell. I don't believe, however, that any group enlivened it or entertained it more than the Big Blue Society.

Nobody knew how long Site 45 had been maintained by the New York Department of Parks and Recreation. We did know, however, that there was a scarcity of firewood. This did not impede the Blues. In late afternoon, we fanned out and ranged several hundred yards in search of wood. Large branches, fallen deadwood and uprooted stumps formed an impressive pile of fuel. In the evening, after dinner, the fire would grow to become a bonfire. It would routinely burn for most of the night. Each day, we would repeat the exercise of gathering wood.

We fished that evening with little luck. Only Lyle managed to catch a small bass that he meticulously prepared for his evening meal. Some of us thought that he flaunted his limited success and seemed to particularly savor each mouthful. It would come back to haunt him.

Following the evening meal, we gathered around the fire. Coolers were drawn close as the evening chill settled in with the darkness. The small cook fire expanded as we took turns feeding it. Conversation and alcohol flowed freely and Bobby lit three joints in succession. He toked deeply from each, provoking a long coughing fit and passed the joints at random. Someone asked Lyle if going on the trip caused problems with his wife. Lyle leaned back, exhaled a plume of smoke and responded that it didn't much matter because he was always in the doghouse. It was just a matter of size.

Maypo brought up the topic of elections. It had been a year since he was disqualified from office, a year in which we were without a leader. Maypo voiced his concern and we all agreed that election should be held, but we put it off for the following night around the campfire.

"That's good," Lyle muttered.

"Why is that good?" I inquired.

"Because I might be interested in running for office."

His response was greeted with laughter and Lyle seemed offended. "Someone have a problem with me running for president?" he asked.

"Not at all," Bob assured him with a chuckle, as he passed yet another joint.

As the evening progressed, it became apparent that Bobby had decided that this was his night to howl. I'd observed my fellow Blues on past Rendezvous. Seldom did we all get completely wasted at the same time. Without planning it we seemed to pass the torch of total inebriation from member to member. We all overindulged at one time or another on Rendezvous and the Bob man had claimed this night.

Empty beer cans piled up at his feet. He practically chain-smoked several joints and he periodically rose from his cooler only to pour himself a shot of Ron Rico Rum. It was on one of these brief excursions that Bob performed his imitation of Joan of Arc. While unsteadily passing by the fire, Bob managed to fall into it. Our initial reaction was not immediate. Our reflexes slowed by pot and alcohol, we watched him flounder for a few seconds like a stuck pig at a barbecue. Eventually, we simultaneously roused ourselves and assisted a sputtering Bobby from the flames. His clothing had just begun to catch. We patted him down and settled him on his cooler. Bob claimed to have tripped, but the way I remember it was that he paused by the fire and seemed to be mesmerized by the flames. At one point he simply fell in.

Years later, Bob was assigned the task of amending Bobby's Rules of Order. There was an addendum to a section regarding "the camp-fire." It read something to the effect that there would always be a bucket of water close to the fire. I recall asking him if this was an effort to prevent a forest fire.

"Fuck, no," he responded. "It's to douse me if I ever fall in the mother fucker again!"

Long after midnight, as the fire began to burn down, we heard an engine on the lake. We listened to it draw close to our site. Eventually the engine cut-out and we made our way unsteadily to the shore. We were greeted by our smiling brother-in-law, Pouncer. He earned his Society name at a lavish family event celebrating our parent's 50th wedding anniversary. A mouse scooted across the head table and Pouncer dove at it just before it jumped into my mother's fondue. He trapped it in his linen napkin and, with quiet dignity, squeezed it lifeless. He had the style of a Blue. We had no idea he was coming to the Rendezvous. All he knew was that we were camping somewhere on the fifteen or so miles of Lower Saranac shore.

"How the fuck did you find us?" Maypo asked.

"Are you kidding? I could hear you guys laughing three miles away."

*Bobby, Lyle, Sausage, Pouncer, Fresh
Meat, Whippo, Buck, Cosmos*

The next morning, all except Bobby went fishing. Bob didn't emerge from his tent until mid-morning. When he finally did, he complained about his hangover and superficial burns on his hands.

Once again that morning the fish did not cooperate. We discussed lures, techniques and promising locations over a late breakfast. We had been vaguely aware of a boat that had anchored a short while earlier not more than fifty feet off our site. We'd paid little attention to the boat or the two occupants. Suddenly, however, we were roused by energetic shouts coming from the boat. We moved toward the shore as a group and made our way out onto the granite ledge that extended about sixty feet into the lake. One of the men in the boat was bent over the side. When he straightened up, he was holding a pike that must have been three feet long.

"That pike is bigger than my dick!" Fresh Meat said.

Whippo corrected him by saying, "That pike's tail is bigger than your dick."

Fresh Meat smiled at his father in acknowledgment.

We watched silently for a few minutes as the second man quickly landed a second pike equal in size. We chafed with insult. These were, after all, in our minds, territorial waters. Where we had been unsuccessful earlier that morning, these fellows were hauling out trophy pike right by our doorstep.

"Where you fellas from?" Maypo called to them.

They seemed surprised at the sound of his voice. Perhaps they had been so engrossed in fishing that they hadn't noticed us. They looked up together and beheld eight scruffy, wood stained, bleary-eyed Blues whose body language suggested a collective instability.

"Well, boys, we're up from New Jersey for a little fishing."

"No shit," Lyle dead-panned to Maypo.

We didn't respond and the silence hung like a weight suspended over the fifty feet that separated us.

"So where you boys all from?" the fisherman asked.

"Well," Bob said, "We're all from Rhode Island. We're the fucking Big Blue Society."

As Bobby spoke, we noticed he was unbuckling his belt. The signal from Bob passed from man to man like a Rockettes chorus line. One after another, pants met ankles and we collectively turned our backsides to our new acquaintances. As we bent deeply and aggressively grasped our white asses, Maypo informed the trespassers that this was The Big Blue's way of saying hello. Equally discernible in the gesture was that it was also our way of saying good-bye. By the time we had refastened our belts, they were starting their motor. We didn't see them again.

That afternoon, following lunch, I sat on the edge of the lean-to and entertained myself by plunking beer cans with Pouncer's pellet gun. I was on my fourth beer and I'd smoked the better part of a joint. This isn't me, I thought, as I stepped outside my considerable buzz. I don't do this in the middle of a weekday afternoon. But it was me. Like a drowning man straining to reach the surface, something deep inside me aspired to the earthy essence that was at the heart of the Big Blue Society. There was something in the way of raw unspoken attraction that drew me to this group. These were men who embraced the idea of casting a collective four-day moon at an all too politically correct society. A society that exerted a stronger influence over us than we cared to admit.

At one point, Bobby joined me and challenged me to a target-shooting contest. A few feet away, a brisk horseshoe game pitted Buck and Cosmos against Maypo and Lyle. I wasn't a bad shot, but I was no competition for the Bob-man and we both knew it. After his first tour in Viet Nam, following high school, Bob was reassigned to a R. I. Nike Missile Site. We spent a great deal of time together that summer. Periodically, I would go to his house and occasionally Bob would remove a .22 rifle from a gun rack in his room. I would watch in awe as Bob would pop small birds in flight from his bedroom window. The adrenaline was heightened by the fact that Bob lived in a densely settled sub-division.

"Bob," I recall asking him, "Isn't that kind of dangerous, firing a twenty-two like that?"

"Not if you don't miss," he had responded.

From twenty-five feet, I watched as Bob routinely hit cigarette butts propped in the tops of empty beer cans. What made this display all the more challenging was the fact that Bob was in the midst of cultivating a meaningful buzz. In boredom, Bob began to seek other targets. Lyle was standing about twenty feet away, deeply engrossed in horseshoes. Bob and I were joined by Whippo and Fresh Meat and we began to analyze Lyle's horseshoe toss. Lyle threw an odd shoe. It wasn't a complete flop, more like a three-quarter. What defined it, however, was the Body English Lyle applied once the horseshoe left his hand. Lyle became a caricature of his toss, mimicking its flight with his body contortions, attempting to influence its trajectory. The effect was geometrically increased relative to the amount of alcohol Lyle consumed.

Lyle interrupted each turn by nursing a beer that rested on a nearby stump. Having observed this, Bob casually blew two holes in Lyle's beer can. Lyle returned to his beer, hoisted it, and seemed unaware of the brew rolling down his chest before it reached his mouth. In fact, Lyle retrieved a second beer and the exercise was repeated only Bob shot a hole through the can while Lyle was holding it. Whippo, Fresh Meat, Pouncer and Bobby howled with laughter. Periodically, Lyle would cast a challenging look our way. In his compromised condition, he thought we were laughing at his horseshoe toss.

As the game wore on, our attention was diverted to Cosmos. His shoes no longer were close to the stake. In fact, they were landing in the bushes, several yards from the target. Cosmos had brought along a couple of bottles of tequila. Around ten that morning, he had christened a bottle. There was very little left. Cosmos began to sway even more than Lyle after each shot. After one particularly off-target heave, his sideways momentum propelled him through the bushes towards the water like a crazed moose in search of a mate. He landed on his back at the edge of the lake and convulsed with laughter, paralyzed by his own predicament. Eventually he rose, unsteadily peeled off his clothing and struck out bare-assed for a rocky point a few hundred yards away.

Cosmos' action abruptly halted the horseshoes and we moved to the ledge as a group. Clothes came off and we swam naked in the dark water. Maypo attempted to find the bottom but was unsuccessful. He reported that the deeper he went the colder and darker it became.

After a few minutes we returned to the ledge and observed Cosmos making steady progress towards the opposite shore. It was at that time that we saw a boat approaching in the distance. As the boat drew near, we remained on the ledge and wrapped towels across our mid-sections. Cosmos was only a few feet from the opposite shore as the boat slowly passed our point. Two elderly couples smiled and waved enthusiastically. We were hoping that Cosmos would have the sense to remain in the water. In true Blue fashion, he did just the opposite. We watched as he emerged quickly from the water, gingerly stepping on the slick moss-covered rocks in an effort to gain the cover of the woods. The boaters had yet to notice him. He seemed to hesitate momentarily and rather than walk along the shore to find an opening into the woods, Cosmos decided to scale the twenty-foot rock in front of him. The rest of us repeatedly waved to the couples in the boat in an effort to divert their attention from Cosmos. We were, however, unsuccessful.

One of the women spotted Cosmos and yelped, "Oh, my God!" thus alerting the others.

Cosmos had managed to scamper halfway up the rock, but now had nowhere to go. He reminded me of a skinny, white monkey that was attached to a mobile that had hung over my daughter's crib years ago. Cosmos seemed to panic and he dropped like a swatted fly back into the water. The boat moved on and despite Bob's efforts to get them to wave again, they refused. Perhaps it was because the ladies' hands were stuck to their mouths in disbelief.

Eventually, Cosmos made the return swim. He was tired, still drunk and a trickle of blood ran down his nose. He offered no apology.

That night, as promised, we held elections. Maypo nominated Lyle because, he explained, there was nothing about Lyle that was not a good fit for the society. He was laid back, irresponsible, drank too much on Rendezvous and was frequently out of favor with his wife. What was not to like? Bobby and I fought it but we were eventually worn down by the illogical and consequently highly effective arguments of Maypo, Cosmos and Whippo. Pouncer and Fresh Meat attempted to chime in, but the Bob man reminded them, "On your first Rendezvous, you don't get to say diddly about something as important as the election of the Grand Scrotum."

So, Lyle became our president on Wednesday night. He had diligently pursued the office for more than twenty years and now he sat on his cooler in the gathering darkness, flush with his achievement. He repeatedly flashed the presidential salute and poured himself a small pitcher of scotch to embellish his victory. Lyle drank the scotch in several quick gulps. He expelled the air in his lungs with a hearty burp and fixed each man in turn with a glassy-eyed stare. Bob sat next to me on my oversized cooler.

"It's starting," he said.

"What?" I asked.

"His fucking lip is on its way to his chin."

Lyle decided that he would celebrate his victory with his best meal of the trip. To his credit, Lyle took camp cooking seriously. He was not content with simply a piece of chicken, fish or steak and perhaps a potato. Lyle was a frustrated Gourmand. He reminded me of a mechanic with the finest tools. The only problem was that he didn't know how to use them. Out of his cooler came a large white package. A can of corn joined it on the picnic table and a foil-wrapped pouch suggested a potato. Lyle by now was feeling the full effect of a daylong binge, fueled by the nervousness associated with elections. The voluminous victory scotch had not helped him. He slowly unwrapped the white package and withdrew a steak the size of a small Buick. He held it up like a magician with a rabbit that magically appeared from a hat.

There was something wrong about the steak. I remember, but at the moment I couldn't figure out what it was. Lyle, holding his steak like a trophy, moved unsteadily towards the fire and placed the meat on the edge of the grill. A small problem confronting Lyle was the wide gap between grilling slats. He no sooner placed the steak on the grill than I knew what was wrong with his meat. It was impressive in its width. Perhaps it was eight or nine-inches square, but it was only the thickness of a shirt cardboard. The hot grill performed a magic trick of its own with Lyle's steak. It immediately sizzled and curled the edges, causing the steak to fold in upon itself and fall in a heap through the slats into the fire.

Lyle, upon seeing this, panicked while the rest of us began to laugh. He attempted to rescue the steak, but only managed to poke it deeper into the coals. It was Cosmos, serving as his sous chef, who managed to pluck the meat from the flames, burning his fingers in the process. With the meat back safely on the grill, although now half its original size, Lyle turned his attention to his cream corn. He opened it with some difficulty and placed it on the edge of the fireplace to warm. Sometime earlier, his foil-wrapped potato had been swallowed by the coals.

At this point, Lyle again tended his prize cut of beef. He attempted to turn the rapidly charring steak and in the process dumped it back into the fire. This time, nobody offered to help him. We couldn't move because we were so convulsed with laughter.

I recall Bobby's laugh. Step one was a chuckle, step two turned into a belly laugh, and the final stage was a muffled wheezing and a lot of shaking of the cooler on which we both sat. The more Lyle struggled to salvage his meat, the more we laughed. He finally managed to extract the burnt offering that now resembled a hockey puck and placed it on his plate. He wobbled towards his can of cream corn and burned his fingers trying to pick it up. This action almost caused a third plunge of his steak back into the fire. Lyle eventually managed to deposit the corn on his plate and began to move behind us to his own cooler. Each unsteady step deposited a few kernels of corn on the ground. He reminded me of Hansel and Gretel who dropped bread in the forest in hopes of finding their way home.

There was one root on the way to Lyle's cooler that lay in wait for this unsteady traveler. Lyle was within feet of the sanctuary of his cooler when he hit it. Lyle stumbled but managed not to fall. The steak and most of the corn were not as fortunate. Lyle plopped on his cooler and looked mournfully at his plate. The steak was somewhere in the darkness and only a small amount of corn remained on his plate. Pouncer walked over and placed a small, crinkled pouch of aluminum foil on his plate.

"You forgot this," he said.

Early the following morning, Bob and I fished the weed bed off our site. We hoped to duplicate the success of the New Jersey anglers from the previous day. Bob was cranky and out of sorts. This was unusual for Bob who usually brimmed with optimism. I queried him between casts in an effort to plumb his mood. He was evasive and seemed to wrap himself in the silence of his hangover. I could elicit only an occasional grunt. I concentrated on fishing and let the emerging sun warm my back. At one point I thought I was snagged on a weed bed, but my line suddenly surged to the left, accompanied by the whine of my drag. I could feel a weight to the fish that suggested it could be big. I alerted Bob and he quickly reeled his line in. After a couple of minutes, as the fish drew near the boat, it flashed, revealing a pike the size of my arm. The pike broke Bobby's silence.

"Did you see the size of that fucking thing?" he asked.

I maneuvered the fish alongside, feeling my heart thud in my chest. I told Bob to get the net ready. I could see my treble hook lodged precariously in the pike's snout.

"Net him how, Bob!" I instructed, fearful of losing my prize.

Bob leaned over the side of the boat and I watched in horror as he attempted to slide the net over the head of the fish. Before I could say anything, the net dislodged the hook from the pike's mouth. He splashed once, dousing Bob's head and torso and disappeared into the black water.

"Fuck, Bob!" I said, drilling him with an intense stare. "You don't net a fish from the front!"

He scanned out across the water in an effort to avoid looking at me and said, "Man, what the fuck do I know about fishing?"

It was Bob's way of admitting his mistake and I accepted it as an apology. I checked my lure and resumed fishing. Neither of us spoke. The only sounds were the click of a bail, the splash or a spoon and the soft whine of the retrieve. Eventually, Bob interrupted the silence with a muttered expletive.

"What was that?" I coaxed him.

"Fuckin' Lyle," he responded more distinctly. "Can you believe that sorry-assed motherfucker is our president?" he continued.

I watched as Bob churned himself into a lather. "Is that what you're so pissed off about?" I asked.

"Fucking A," he spit. "Did you see him last night after he won the election? I think we should charge him with F & F."

"Let me guess. Would that be Fornication and Fellatio?" I asked.

"No," Bob responded in the midst of a long cast. "Flaunting and Flashing."

"What do you mean?" I inquired.

"Sausage, give me a break. You saw him last night. Now he's the president, so he struts around like a lovesick turkey. He sucks up that fucking lip and hangs his dick out the side of his shorts about twenty times an hour." Bob took two deep hits from his cigarette and tossed the butt in the water. "Don't tell Cosmos I did that," he said. Bob was on a roll now.

"Did you see that motherfucker try to cook dinner? It was a disgrace. And this sorry specimen of humanity is now our president, the Grand Fucking Scrotum? I'm personally embarrassed."

Bobby and Sausage

Kingmakers

"Well, Bob," I cajoled. "There's very little we or anybody else can do now."

The silence settled briefly.

"I wouldn't exactly say there's nothing we can do about it!" Bob suddenly exclaimed.

I looked at him but said nothing, waiting for him to elaborate.

"We could fucking impeach him," Bob said, summoning that infamous impish grin.

The afternoon of our final day, the sun-dappled campsite served as a stage for men at play. Horseshoes and target shooting blurred into swimming and sunbathing. In twilight, we gathered around the fire for the final time. An assortment of leftovers graced the grill. Chicken vied with sausage and steak for space. Much of our energy had been sapped by the combination of physical exertion laced with pot and alcohol. I studied the faces of my fellow Blues. None had shaved in four days. Cosmos was sporting a red-bristled growth that matched his blood-shot eyes and the crusty scab on his nose. Fresh Meat, still smiling, wore the same t-shirt he had arrived in. Now it was mottled with grease and food stains. Bob had not changed any of his clothes in four days.

"Fuck it," he explained when I asked him about it. "When I get home, I'll just strip down and burn the motherfuckers."

Dr. El Whippo sat on a cooler and picked meticulously at his toenails. Periodically, he would rise and tend his chicken with the same loving care he had lavished on his toenails. Maypo and Pouncer were absorbed in quiet conversation off to the side.

It was Lyle, however, who drew my attention. He appeared smug and self-confident. He was seemingly wrapped in the cocoon of his election victory as he perched precariously on his cooler. He reminded me of a rooster in the hen house as I watched him glance around the encampment. Wherever his eyes settled, I imagined him thinking that "Ah, yes. To the victor goes the spoils." He was officially the Grand Scrotum. He produced a Marlboro from his vest pocket and lit it with an ember. He tilted back and lifted his chin, exhaling into the night. I glanced at Bob who deflected my gaze with a wink. Lyle asked Maypo to fetch him yet another beer. The Grand Scrotum seemed to be driven by a cranky engine. At times lethargic and sputtering. Occasionally purring like a preened cat. In essence, as whimsical as the weather. The only constant was the required fuel. Pure unadulterated alcohol. In the last few hours, still aglow from the previous night, Lyle had dedicated himself to engine maintenance.

The incessant daytime chatter of the red squirrels was squelched by the blanket of nightfall. The sounds were timelier. As long as there had been fire and men to warm themselves by it, the sounds were the same. Farts and belches. Muffled conversation and the snap of a burning log. The Blues serenaded each other and added the pop of a beer can for percussion.

At one point, El Whippo inquired of Lyle where we might be going for next year's Rendezvous.

"I haven't decided yet," Lyle informed him. "But you can be sure that as your president I will give it careful consideration."

Lyle's cavalier attitude, tinged with false ego spurred the Bob-man to action. He rose from his cooler and approached the fire. For the next few minutes, he furiously fed the fire with anything flammable that he could lay his hands on. Lyle was forced to retreat from the growing flames. Finally Bobby, expended by his labors, flopped on his cooler next to Lyle. He scratched aimlessly in the dirt with a thin branch.

"Lyle, let me ask you something. Have you ever heard of Rule 15 in Bobby's Rules of Order?"

"Nope," Lyle responded, staring into the fire.

"It has to do with defiling the campsite."

Lyle turned towards Bobby, who was now a magnet for our collective attention.

"So?" Lyle said, prompting Bob to continue.

"Well," Bob said, his voice rising like a barrister trying to etch a point into the collective mind of a jury. "What the fuck do you call this?"

Bob rose and slowly turned, letting his hand sweep around the darkened campsite. Clumps of corn, camouflaged by daytime sunlight and pine needles, now looked different. The mixture of light and shadow cast from Bobby's bonfire exposed the corn like pearls on a necklace. Everywhere in the darkness corn kernels glowed like embers, pointing their accusatory fingers at Lyle. Lyle, like a leopard denying his spots, shrunk a little lower on his cooler and pulled his ball cap a notch closer to his nose. He said nothing in response.

Bob fired the next volley. "I believe that constitutes grounds for impeachment."

"You've got to be fucking kidding?" Lyle yelped, rising from his cooler.

"I'm afraid I'm serious," Bob deadpanned. "I vote we impeach this sorry-assed motherfucker."

"I'll go along with that," I heard myself say.

"Yep, me too," Cosmos said from somewhere in the darkness.

"You won't get any argument here," Maypo joined in.

"Is it unanimous?" Buck asked.

"Count me in," El Whippo piped up.

"Me too," his son added.

"Shut up, Fresh Meat! You aren't eligible to vote," Lyle managed to stammer through shock and disbelief.

It happened with the suddenness of a car wreck. Lyle slumped in disbelief.

"Well, I guess this means we no longer have a president," I declared.

"I nominate Bobby," Buck said with enthusiasm, rising from his cooler for the first time in hours.

"I accept!" Bob responded.

"You got my vote," I said. "All in favor?" I inquired.

A chorus of "ayes" greeted me. Shortly thereafter, slowly, unsteadily, giddy with laughter and aided by flashlights, we made our way to the rocky peninsula. The moon was nearly full and its soft light defined and blended the grays and blacks of the water, rocks and woods on the opposite shore. We lapsed into silence, spread out on the rocks like Lyle's corn. We soaked up the night and let it caress us. Lyle sat on the edge about thirty feet above the water. Like a praying mantis who had stopped praying, he was folded at an odd angle. His long, bony knees were drawn up to his chin. His hands dangled at his side and only the top of his head was visible between his knees. His beer had tipped over and his sneaker was marinating in the puddle. Occasionally, he would twitch and threaten to topple into the water.

"Lyle," someone muttered, "I think it's time for bed."

His head appeared slowly and he rose in sections. He balanced unsteadily and peered around like a drunk awakening in a strange room. His lip hung to the bottom of his chin. "Where's my tent?" he asked nobody in particular.

Bob reached for his flashlight, snapped it on and pointed to the path.

"Over there," he said, and immediately extinguished the beacon.

That image of Lyle, water, rocks and moonlight and a foiled guidance system will forever be my last image of that Rendezvous. I watched as Lyle inched across the rock towards the path. I wondered if this was how Dewey felt the morning after losing to Truman.

Sausage and Buck

The better part of one's life consists of his friendships.

ABRAHAM LINCOLN

BUCK'S PLACE

The upside of a messy mid-life is you get to reinvent yourself. I quit teaching high school and volunteered at the orphanage Whippo grew up in. It put me in touch with Lamar, a five-year-old boy with honey brown skin, a carpet of curls, and a smile that belied a sucky life. I took him out a few times to the movies and a video arcade, but his favorite place was the lake. He loved to stand on the dock with his life jacket on and cast about for bluegills. One day, he caught a bass and it was magic. He hugged me so tight we nearly fell in the water. I knew in that moment that we could be family.

Lamar's social worker wanted to take things slowly, but a month later I was the foster parent of a special needs boy, dealing with behavior problems at home, and championing his cause at school. It was a lot to take care of and I needed a break, but I could only get away for a night or two. Then Buck extended the perfect invite: if Blues could not leave the home front, then the home front would come to them.

Bobby was living in Hartford with his 3rd wife and their two-year-old daughter. He had moved from Texas in response to a homing instinct. He missed the Northeast with its change of seasons, and he wanted to be near family and friends. Sausage parlayed Buck's invitation into a two-day Rendezvous. **Bobby remembers it this way.**

I WAS SITTING IN my Hartford office at the D.A.V. when the direct line to my desk rang. The Sausage was on the other end, baiting me with the call for a Rendezvous.

"Bob," he says, "you're not gonna fucking believe this."

"I'm curious. Where and when?" I asked.

"Next week," he blurts out accompanied by a chuckle.

"Perfect. My wife and daughter are going to Houston. Where are we going?"

"Nowhere," was followed by a pause, a sufficient block of time by which to imagine all kinds of possibilities. Naturally my first thought was of the reservoir. But surely Sausage could not be thinking of such a bold undertaking. He had left me to dangle just long enough.

"Bob, we're going back to the reservoir, sort of."

I was confused, the anxiety building in my bones. Sausage went on to explain that Buck, the least likely candidate to do anything constructive for the Blue, had made amends for his 10-year reign of mediocrity. Buck had accomplished what only one other man in Rhode Island history had retained. He had purchased a feeder lake for the Swansicut Reservoir System. Hidden from mere mortals like us, this spring fed marvel was set high on a hill. It was flanked on all sides by thick woods and ever higher elevations of granite ledge. Giant pines lined the shore, a soft summer breeze whispered through their long needles. Hearty bullfrogs bellowed their nocturnal songs, dragon flies sped from one water lily to another, and only an occasional large-mouth bass broke the tranquility in search of a fat fly for his dinner.

I had to hand it to the Sausage, he could turn a phrase. This guy could sell pocket warmers at the gates of hell, but I remained skeptical. Afterall, I knew the Sausage for who he really was, a lying whore.

I drove the hour down Route 6 through Connecticut to Swansicut, Rhode Island and pulled into the Sausage's driveway. It was early afternoon. Now the best way to describe his preparation for any

Rendezvous was orderly. His SUV was neatly packed with everything from the rarest bottles of grappa to gourmet meats already iced down in an igloo cooler. Naturally, there were a couple of gizmos that the Sausage had purchased from the Home Shopping Network and the catalog sales department of the 21st century angler. And the Sausage was chomping at the bit.

"Follow me Bob," he yelled.

Jimmy Buffet crooned, "A Pirate Looks at Forty," as we made our way down a long dirt road and approached an 18th century farmhouse flanked by a number of smaller out buildings and a huge rustic barn. I had no idea where the fuck we were going but my skepticism was slowly subsiding. What appeared to be the driveway to this old farm was another dirt road. Several hundred yards later, we drove up on the lake that Sausage had so perfectly described. The spectacular location and scenery became secondary to the sight of my Big Blue brothers. Their tents and camping equipment were strewn about the site. The centerpiece was the framework for a huge campfire and a 10-foot picnic table set beneath a great shade tree at the water's edge. The table was cluttered with vintage bottles of wine, rare and expensive bottles of liquor, and the ever-present herb.

Buck's rainwear

Sausage busied himself by unloading his car, his cache of equipment resembling the river of plenty. I was finished as soon as I started. I grabbed a $15 bottle of Ron Rico rum and a 2-liter bottle of diet coke and headed for the table. I sat, rolled a joint and proceeded to get completely fucked up.

I watched and marveled at the sight of the camp, my brothers setting up in signature style. Each oddly shaped tent was prepared with a drainage ditch in the event of rain. Air mattresses were inflated, sleeping bags were fluffed, and the endless tide of Coleman lanterns, stoves and other essential equipment emerged to find its rightful place. Within the hour, the camp had been set up to everyone's satisfaction and we began about our business in earnest.

Now, you should know that this Rendezvous was to be quite different from our previous getaways. Don't get me wrong. We were bivouacking, but we really hadn't gotten away, which left the door open for visitors and closed somewhat to our inhibitions. Well, for everyone except me. I just don't fucking care. The first real indicator that things would be different came from Shitfish. I hadn't noticed it right away, but old Shitfish had arrived well before Sausage and I. He was set up at the edge of the woods in a self-contained travel trailer, complete with awning, lawn chairs, and all of the apparatus necessary to sustain a small family in the national parks system. Shitfish was turning our annual Rendezvous into a Monty Hall production and behind door number three was a fucking Winnebago.

Maypo, Shitfish, Winnebago

I'm certain that there were others who shared my contempt for this unnatural display, but we had to tread lightly around the Shitfish. His skin was not nearly as tough as the older members and we could not run the risk of hurting his feelings. He provided an invaluable service for the Society by playing the banjo around the campfire and we could ill afford to lose that. Shitfish was, without question, the best banjo player I ever heard, and his melodic blue grass tunes filled a void during those times when the rest of us were too fucked up to function beyond listening.

I could have dwelled on the Winnebago monstrosity but mine and everyone else's attention shifted to the Sausage. Maypo had proclaimed that it was time to test the waters. Expletives flew in the air as each member challenged the fishing competence of another, but no one could have imagined the levity that the Sausage would produce in the next 20 minutes. He approached the shore with his latest contraption. At this point, there was eye contact and a host of smiles. Everyone knew that the Sausage was about to get technical.

A huge green floppy object had reared its ugly head. This thing looked like a cross between the Pillsbury Dough Boy and Moby's dick. The lower assembly was a pair of green boots that rose from the giant mud gripping feet to the bottom of your rib cage. A single full size inner tube ringed the rubbery midriff area and a flack jacket look alike, complete with snap swivels, towing line, and a variety of pockets completed the ensemble.

In principle and according to the directions, the angler dons this Halloween costume, wades in waist deep water where he has sneaked up on some unsuspecting fish and has his way with them. Sausage had rigged the outfit to tow a small cooler of cold ones and a pail of shiners. He stripped naked on the bank. Mind you, the directions don't go there but the Sausage did whenever the opportunity presented itself. He slid into Moby's Dick, grabbed his fishing pole and began to negotiate the rocky shoreline. Between the tow lines, the rocks and soft bottom, the Sausage crashed and burned. He was ass over elbows in three feet of water. The Shiners spilled and were sucked into Moby's dick by the great surge of water rushing into the giant rubber vacuum.

"He's down, he's up, he's fucked up!"

The laughter was of the deep belly variety and sustained. A normal man would have crawled back to shore, swallowed his pride and lived to fish another day, but not our Sausage. Determined to stave off his embarrassment, he righted himself, moved deeper into the lake and began a series of geometric casts. At this point the shiners, trapped inside his rubber nightmare, were frantically swimming in search of an exit.

"Something is attacking my nuts," the Sausage yelled in a panic.

The laughter continued. He made a hasty retreat for the shore falling once more and taking on additional water. He emerged from the lake shedding his latest contraption, shiners flopping about on to the ground. Moby's Dick lay lifeless at the water's edge and Sausage swore in ways I never heard him before.

Lyle pointed an accusatory finger and charged that the Sausage was engaged in bestiality with the little fish. Sausage answered this charge in the same manner as all other charges levied by Lyle.

"Fuck you Lyle," he said.

Yeah, it was happening. My assault on the lake was euphoric. I landed eight bass in twenty minutes and forged an early lead in the fishing competition. This fact, although disputed by some, seemed to go up everybody's ass sideways since my accomplishments were always with borrowed equipment and stolen lures. I don't actually bring anything on these trips apart from my sense of humor. I take a lot of heat for my lack of preparedness, but I pass it off as a manifestation of my psychiatric malady, a leftover from my second tour in Vietnam. I learned to travel light, be ready at a moment's notice, and deny everything.

Camp was outstanding, revelry at every turn. As I look back on things and remember, I'm left with one resolve, "Camp is my friend". In many ways, this camp was especially dear to my heart. It wasn't so much that it was Buck's and that he was sharing his little piece of nature with us, but moreover where it was. I felt for the first time in many years that I was actually home. It was the Swansicut Reservoir and yet it wasn't. Regardless, it sure felt like home.

The second night around the campfire was the best ever. We were honored with a visit from a longtime friend and associate member, Kevin "Cornbread" Feely. He was a funny little prick, the kind of guy who sees the humor in everything. He could have a good time if he were locked in a closet. I think that's what I admired most about him. He was in the middle of a mid-life catastrophe but only because he let it get way beyond a crisis. He dyed his gray hair gold and moussed them up on top of his head in a style befitting guys half his age. He spent his time at pooty bars and his pursuit of the legendary holy mackerel was approaching shameful proportions.

Cornbread was the horniest man in the world. He defended his status with a morality tale that most men can relate to. "Say you live your life as a complete dickwad. You hit on everything that moves and then you die. You go to judgment and God opens the book. He flips through pages of transgressions and smiles. 'Not bad,' He says. 'I made you the horniest man in the world. You could have done a lot worse. Come on in.'" That was Cornbread's tale. The point is, you never know exactly where you stand in the big picture. The Big Blue feel this way about our get-outs in the woods. We go for it because it's in us. Will it be held against us in the end? Only God knows.

The Sausage surprised everyone with a ten-pound tenderloin of beef for dinner. I can't remember the side dishes with any detail but I'm sure they had something to do with herbs, harps, barley and any other grains that you could think of. The beef was the best I had ever tasted. It was devoured in true Blue fashion and no sooner had the last paper plate been thrown into the fire then the lying and farting began. Now Cornbread, who is not much of a farter, at least not up to my thunderous standards, can lie with the best of us. He was a welcome addition on this fine summer night.

Sausage almost always gets the campfire chatter rolling and more often than not in a shameful direction. He began with his customary lead, "Bob, tell us, did you ever fuck anyone who read a comic book and ate an apple while you were doing them?"

"Only once," I replied.

"Tell us about it, Bob."

This type of carefully phrased question would lead the conclave to new lows. The Oracle of the Obvious had struck again. Sausage knew exactly where to take these fireside chats and he reveled in the entertainment. Once again, I was shamed into telling the story of the Saigon whore who compromised my masculinity and left me to flounder in sexual no man's land. At the tender age of 18, she had destroyed my Don Juan psyche at the expense of her appetite for fruit and her lust for a laugh. I reminded everyone that she had only managed one bite from the apple before I snatched the comic book, took a bite from her apple, rolled her over and took her down a new highway of adventure. Saigon Sally would not be so carefree in the future, I was sure.

Each funny story, each joke reminded us of another. The hours passed, the laughter building in harmony with our respective buzz. The conversation circled the fire. And somewhere in the madness, I brought up my anticipated move back to Houston.

"Are you being transferred?" Sausage asked.

"No! I'm going to retire and maybe try my hand at small business."

"What do you have in mind?" Cornbread sounded genuinely interested. I guess it was his business background that sparked his curiosity. The rest of the guys knew me too well to take anything I said seriously.

"Oh, I don't know for sure," I said. "I might try my hand at an assortment of products from the "Dick Nose" collection. Dick Nose was my entrepreneurial call sign. I had developed a logo with a man's face and a giant nose in the shape of a penis. I thought the whole concept was catchy.

"Dick Nose Fishing, Dick Nose Golf, something along those lines," I added.

Sausage interrupted, "Bob, you are fucking certifiable." The Oracle of the Obvious had struck again. At this point I introduced the notion of a Hasty Tasty Douche and Lube.

"Now that's a novel idea," Lyle said. "Tell me more."

We had finally touched on a subject with which Cornbread had some level of expertise - pooty! The douche and lube had struck a chord and everyone was hysterical at the thought. I explained that the need for lube jobs was a foregone conclusion. Women from all walks of our society were taking advantage of these quick first echelon operations and that it was my civic duty to take the concept to a new level. Why should Quick Car Care and Jiffy Lube waiting rooms be jammed with women waiting for the family automobile? These waiting rooms offered magazines like Popular Mechanics, Outdoor Life and Sports Illustrated. They were often devoid of conversation and the TV, if there was one, was more often than not tuned to the Winston Cup series or some form of Indy car racing. Cornbread agreed that we should provide a service specifically for the tender gender.

"Service the female chassis," he argued. "A fragrant and refreshing douche while you wait."

I had studied the demographics. The need was apparent, and the conversion was simple as adding a pair of stirrups and employing a douche master. The possibilities were mind boggling. Cornbread provided further evidence of what the Douche and Lube might remedy by way of some recent cunnilingus adventures. He proposed a campaign to endorse legislation that would require douches on a regular basis.

"Make it the law of the land," he said quite forcefully. "I recently dated a woman who was being followed by a flock of seagulls. She reminded me of a fishing boat on its way back into Galilee."

Galilee is Rhode Island's most popular fishing port. It can get rather aromatic in the late afternoon. That Cornbread was dating a woman who reminded him of this North Atlantic fishing village came as no surprise to me. I had been, more than once, where this wonderful and funny little guy was right now. He was reborn. He had rediscovered the holy mackerel and in the process had become somewhat of a pervert. The guy would pay a buck to watch a couple of dogs fuck. Once again, that's what I admired about him.

"Tempus Fugit."

Maypo would throw out these little reminders from the Latin vernacular. Time flies when you're having fun. It was really late. Cornbread, who planned to have only a beer and something to eat, was at least three hours late for his date. We were all drunk or high or both and the night was claiming victims. Shitfish sneaked off to the comfort of his Winnebago. One by one the Blues found their way to the tents that dotted the shoreline. None staged so grand an exit as Lyle. Fifty yards from the campfire, Lyle tripped over Moby's Dick still lying lifeless at the water's edge.

"Mother fucker!" echoed out across the lake.

The accompanying Big Blue laughter slowly gave way to the bull frogs' nocturnal songs. There were a number of other funny moments although most of these are better left buried deep within the Blue Archives. What we know following this trip is that I moved back to Houston and became the proud owner of the only Douche and Lube now operating in the free world. The Big green floppy object known as Moby's Dick disappeared and has not been seen except by Maypo who claims that it hangs in the rafters of Lyle's garage. The only other certainty is that the Blue will endure. We will meet again, and those meetings will serve as the basis for chapters yet to be written.

"There you go again, Bob," I complained over the phone. "Leaving things out that need to be said."

"Maypo, I'm sitting here with the love of my life and everything's good. My little girl's making mud pies and I'm her hero. Someday, she might read this book, and I don't want her thinking I was complete fuck up."

"But Bob, you are. We all are."

"That's beside the point. Some things are best left unsaid."

"You won't write it?"

There was a long silence. I imagined Bob drawing a Marlboro out of a soft pack with his cracked lips.

"I'll see what I can do," he said.

It is impossible to escape the prodding's of a Sullivan. They are a relentless breed. Each dramatically different from one another and yet each quite alike. Maypo is a precious man, sensitive but hard. He is the dreamer of the clan and by far the one most influenced by the moon. Yes, he's a fucking lunatic like myself. You could say that we are frequently on the same page, which doesn't speak well for Maypo. But as a result, he knows how to goad my intellect. He called today. It was like a Paul Harvey flashback.

"Okay, Bob. Time for the rest of the story."

He was referring of course to those moments which belong buried in the Big Blue archive. I resist such challenges to the best of my ability, content to sit around on what is left of my ass and enjoy retirement. But once again, I have been shamed into telling all.

I have often wondered why we do the things we do on Rendezvous. Almost always it comes down to the influences of our world. Afterall, we are the 60's generation, the same generation that gave way to Timothy Leary, Jimi Hendrix, Max Yeager's Farm, Viet Nam, and draft registration. Our heroes were killing themselves at an alarming rate and not even Superman was safe. Our president was murdered for the whole world to see and there was even a guy playing golf on the moon. Now, while all this was taking place, the only creatures who didn't seem to mind were those that lived in the forest. The rest of us were in shock, or just plain fucked-up, but definitely one or the other. The rest of the story concerns the latter.

Everyone gets fucked-up on Rendezvous. The choice rests in how one attains this station. For the most part, alcohol is the drug of choice. However, pot almost always finds its way to our campfire. Occasionally, some other substance will emerge, leaving the Blues to wrestle with their respective consciences. Maypo and I have never wrestled very much. We simply yield to the law of nature that we adopted many years ago while traversing the fire roads around the Swansicut. It was probably back in the Question of Balance time frame that we adopted the philosophy, "If it's good enough for God's creatures, it's good enough for us."

I learned in the Army that we could survive without rations simply by eating what the animals ate. If it didn't kill the animals, it probably wouldn't kill us. This is true for some of the banned substances. For example, I observed on more than one occasion water buffalo ingesting large quantities of cannabis which grew wild in the Viet Nam countryside. I concluded from my observation that one would have to be completely fucked-up to romp around in a rice paddy all day while pulling a plow. Maypo on the other hand had observed certain species of birds and our cute furry friends eating mushrooms which seemed plentiful around the local New England farms. He had studied up on the caps, done spore samples, and was quite confident in his ability to identify edible varieties from poisonous ones. He was particularly interested in a little brown mushroom he claimed had psychotropic properties. When he found a few growing in Buck's woods, he filled a baggy with pieces and stems.

Now this was a new experience for many of the Blues and, once again, not everyone participated. For those who did, the afternoon of the second day was, to say the least, interesting and, at times, hilarious. Maypo announced the beginning of "happy hour" as differentiated from cocktail hour. Maypo and I were first in the bag, followed by

Cosmos, Lyle, and the Sausage. Shitfish stared in disbelief. He had eaten a lot of strange things in his day, but he wasn't about to ingest something that was potentially toxic. Buck poured himself a generous glass of Jim Beam and sat back to take in the show.

Our excitement built as we waited to see which of the shroom people would be the first to realize the effects. I couldn't say how long it took, but Sausage was definitely first. His eyeballs began canvassing the sky, each cloud formation representing some historic figure. He was clearly uncomfortable with seeing the likes of Abraham Lincoln and Bozo the Clown and announced that he was going to lie down. Maypo and I chuckled, knowing that any such attempt was futile. Sausage crawled into his tent, zipped the flap, and re-emerged within a minute, beads of sweat affixed to his brow.

"I can't sleep," he exclaimed.

No shit, I thought to myself. I tried, with the help of Maypo, to lure Sausage to our horse pit but it was too late. He had fallen victim to the psychotropic nature of the fungi. Sausage repeated his comical retreat to and from his tent several times, only to be interrupted by Dick Diggle, who arrived in need of signatures on various Sullivan company paychecks. Sensing our general state of incapacity, I believe Dick understood how we destroyed his tent on our first fishing trip. Sausage had no idea how to sign his name let alone deal with an employee. He scrawled his John Hancock in something that looked more like Sanskrit than Palmer method. At this point, he attempted to enlist the help of Buck, but it proved futile. Buck was romancing a bottle of bourbon and laying plans for the next Olympic event. He announced that the Gold Alewife Award would go to the first person who could clean and jerk Lyle's liver. On hearing these details, Lyle went into acute depression and began to resemble the infamous Bottle-lipped Dolphin. To cheer Lyle up, Maypo and I asked him to go for a swim. We stripped down in plain view and slid into the water like muskrats on a slippery bank. Dick left at this point. I'm sure it was an eye-opener to see our white posteriors bobbing up and down in the lake.

It's amazing how one's perspective on things changes with the advent of outside stimuli. Floating there rudderless in the lake, I observed the only thing more appalling than the sight of the fucking Winnebago. It was Shitfish rolling up his awning and hauling his ass away in the monstrosity. It was clear to me that Shitfish wanted nothing to do with the Blues on 'shrooms. I could only imagine he sensed horror at the thought of the Bob-man and a psychotropic initiation.

"Shitfish," Maypo yelled, "Bobby wants you!"

But Shitfish was gone, heading for bluer grass. We were pretty goofy at this point and Maypo was feeling the full effects of his mushroom soufflé. The pupils of his eyes were dilated wide and he complained of shooting pains in his stomach. A few minutes later, he puked in the woods and retired to his tent, ala Sausage. Cosmos seized upon the occasion to play tricks. He hid an expensive walkie-talkie in the leaves beside Maypo's tent and, in varying degrees of urgency, attempted to call forth our deserting brother.

"Maypo," he whispered into the wireless, "get up, get up!"

Indecipherable grunts echoed back from Maypo's tent as his auditory hallucinations took shape. Our collective laughter eventually gave us away and Maypo joined us at the campfire. He described the hi jinx of his mind as being on the corkscrew roller coaster. He kept going round and round, looping inverted, and couldn't get off. He was not having a good time.

"Where's the valium when you need it?" he asked, holding his head.

Nearly everyone agreed that mushrooms should be added to our list of banned substances. Sausage led the call, but the actual vote was a tie. As the presiding Grand Scrotum, Sausage interpreted Shitfish's exodus as a vote in the affirmative. Mushrooms were placed on the list of contraband, never to appear on Big Blue Rendezvous.

Big Tom arrived at sunset carrying a couple of canoe stands he made by hand. He hunked them together from discarded two-by-fours and they were crude but effective. Buck felt bad that Big Tom had not been invited to go on a Rendezvous after the one in Augusta, but he was preserving the Big Fellar from knowing what fuck-ups we really were. And we were still fucked-up at this point. Maypo was drinking Pepto Bismal directly from the bottle. Cosmos was on the walkie-talkie, talking to himself. Sausage was trying to figure out how to cook a hot dog and Lyle was giving him all sorts of shit.

"Where's Whippo?" Big Tom asked.

We didn't know. Had he been invited? Had we forgotten El Whippo? How could we do that? What the hell was wrong with us? Big Tom didn't feel so left out. He opened his tackle box and gave each of us a Hooded Winkle. It was a double treble hook hidden in a hairy cleft of synthetic flesh. It got us all to laughing and Big Tom departed. Buck thanked him for the canoe stands, but as the fire burned down, I dragged one up to the pit. It was a joke of course, but Buck put the stand away knowing I couldn't resist a temptation so close at hand.

BBQ at Buck's

In a final tribute to fungi, the Society commissioned a glockenspiel clock that produces banjo music at midnight. In place of the traditional German dancers, Sausage exits his tent and roams in a mushroom patch. When he bends over to pick one, the Bobman emerges from behind a tree and sneaks up on the Sausage. We do not guarantee the clock's accuracy but hold that its conversational value is priceless.

In God's wilderness lies the hope of the world - the
great, unblighted, unredeemed wilderness.

JOHN MUIR

WESTWARD HO

In the Spring of 1995, Sausage came up with a plan to take the Big Blue on its greatest fishing adventure. He read "A River Runs Through It" and wanted us to experience the unbounded wilderness for ourselves. He booked flights to Billings, Montana, and bought us fly rods and waders. We practiced fly-casting into his swimming pool, and Sausage heralded the 7-day venture as the "trip of a lifetime."

I had my hands full with Lamar so I couldn't go. Bobby passed at the thought of wading in swift rivers with his bad legs. Buck detected that attendance was not mandatory, so he opted to stay home and fish for bass. Whippo's dog had taken ill and Didymus was out. That left Sausage, Cosmos, Shitfish, and Lyle committed to the trip.

Dick Diggle, the guy who loaned Sausage his tent for the first Big Blue trip, and his buddy Rick, had fished out west several times. Sausage invited them come because he needed their fishing intel and experience.

Lyle recounts the trip in which our dubious fishing prowess pursued us across the continent.

S AUSAGE'S WINDOWS WERE frosted, his balls in an uproar. He had become increasingly vexed with the dearth of fish caught on Big Blue trips to the Adirondacks. The recently elected Grand Scrotum decided that the Society must expand its horizons and think on a grander scale. Sausage consulted one of his longtime employees, Dick Diggle, a fly fisherman so obsessed with the sport that throughout the winter months he would hunker down in his basement tying flies for the next season. Every year or so, Dick and his buddy Rick took fly fishing excursions to the great trout waters of Big Sky country, Montana. He would rhapsodize about their successes and assured Sausage that a trip out west was a can't miss proposition. Judging Dick to be of reasonably sound mind and a somewhat responsible fellow (more on this assessment later), Sausage set in motion his extraordinary organizational talents to make the trip happen.

Sausage adroitly completed all the logistics. A trip of this magnitude demanded, at least in his eyes, first class transportation to the airport. Valet service from one of the airport mini vans? Hell no. We were riding in style, a stretch limo baby. Somehow we managed to pack all our gear including rod cases in the trunk and headed off to Cumberland, Rhode Island, which was sort of on the way to Boston, to pick up Shitfish.

You would think that someone who had never ridden in a limo, much less seen one roll into his driveway at 6:30 in the morning to take him fishing, would evoke a greater response from Shitfish other than, "Hey Sausage, do you think there's room in there for this here travel bag?" Assured there was, he followed up with, "Ya know, as you all were pulling in, I thought I heard one them lifters knocking. Before we get on the highway, maybe we should check it out."

Placating Shitfish and his many concerns and/or complaints would prove to a be a daunting task on this trip, but for now we were off and running. International airports, checked baggage, carry-on luggage, rod cases, connecting flights, it all turned into one long travel day. For some reason, I decided to tote around a small Coleman cooler with provisions for emergency situations, be they in terminals, airplanes, boats, or on riverbanks. Naturally, I regretted this decision except for one instance which made the inconvenience of the thing worthwhile. But more on that later.

We arrived in Billings, Montana in the late afternoon expecting to rent a car and be in Yellowstone National Park by dusk. The only problem was that our rod cases had been rerouted to another state and were not scheduled to be in Billings until morning. The seasoned travelers among us demanded and received profuse apologies and promises of recompense from the airlines. Their appeasement offer, a meal voucher and hotel room, was accepted by us rambling rogues. Everyone was tired except me, and I proceeded to hit every bar in downtown Billings, gambled money on slots, and was on a shoestring budget the rest of the trip.

We left for Yellowstone the following morning with Sausage reminding hungover me that "the way of the transgressor sure is rough." We rolled into a small town outside the park to stock up for our initial assault on the rainbows of the Yellowstone River. The prevailing wisdom of the local anglers and bait shop owners was that we needed a fly called the "Sow's Bug." We loaded up on the bug, even Dick and Rick, who had every conceivable fly except that one.

I finished my shopping early and sashayed next door to a souvenir shop. The proprietress was a sultry, strawberry-blond Wyoming cowgirl with a graceful neck that led to square shoulders, breasts that rode high and wide, about the size of large navel oranges, long and lean yet not skinny, a nice small butterball butt, everything that turned on a married guy on a fishing trip like me. I told her that I was separated from my wife back east, my children were grown, and I was seriously considering starting a new life out here in Big Sky country. Dallas Alice seemed intrigued. Then Sausage poked his head in the door and said, "The wagon train is leaving. Have you finished checking out the lady's wares? You can always get something for your wife and kids at the lodge."

Alice gave me a forlorn look that inferred, "Another time, another place." I gave Sausage a look that inferred nothing except, "Thanks a lot, Saus, all I've got is my fantasies."

We checked into our cabins and headed out to the river. The car had barely been shut off when Sausage, Rick, and Cosmos, already in their wading suits, ambled down the banks. By the time Dick, Shitfish and I made it to the river's edge, it looked like April 10th back home on the Wood River. In fact, it was opening day for fishing on the Yellowstone, wall to wall anglers vying for every promising honey hole that could be waded or cast to. Sausage, with typical understatement, glanced over at Dick and said, "Grab a spot Dick, if you can find one."

Dick, grasping all the implications of the simple declarative sentence, started to defend himself. "I didn't know it was opening day Sausage, I've only fished this river once before. You have to admit the scenery is beautiful ain't it?"

Ignoring this lame excuse, Sausage attacked the water with determination and confidence. We fished that river for a day and a half for a total of about 14 hours. The results were dismal with the possible exception of Rick who had the stamina of an ox and an otter's love of water. He waded out into the river early in the morning with nothing but his fly rod and stayed there for 8 hours asking only occasionally for someone to bring him a little water to drink. He caught a total of 16 fish. Sausage caught 4 rainbows and though pleased that he had caught anything, was disillusioned by the extraordinary effort required. Cosmos also managed to land a couple. Shitfish was AWOL most of the time claiming age and infirmary would not allow him to traverse the rapids. He groused away the time fishing in the least promising areas. Often the tranquil stillness of the river was disturbed by a string of invectives emanating from some small tributary around a bend in the river.

"God damn son of a bitch no good fucking whore fly!!!" To which Sausage would inevitably inquire, "Any luck Shitfish?"

"Nah," said Shitfish, "I just lost another Sow Bug, that's all."

I was luckless and skunked, but not for lack of effort. Dick, for all his expertise, managed to catch about 7 fish. He spent a significant portion of his time squatting on the banks, smoking cigarettes, and looking for new insect hatches that were nonexistent. It was in just such a pose that he provided tremendous comic relief for us and helped allay our bruised fishing egos.

As everyone knows, Bison roam freely in Yellowstone Park, often stopping traffic, be it pedestrian or vehicles. Anyone with half a brain knows not to fuck with those big bad boys. Besides being temperamental, they can swim easily across swift rivers, run 25 mph and weigh thousands of pounds. Well, as Dick was leisurely smoking and scanning the water, I was fishing out in the river and spotted a granddaddy of a buffalo, a woolly mammoth size beast, slowly grazing his way over in Dick's direction. We all assumed that Dick would notice it and yield his ground. Meanwhile, I was highly amused at the scene unfolding and said nothing. When Dick still did not notice it, now 15 yards away, I got Dick's attention and started motioning him to look to his right. Dick thought I was cracking on him by pointing out a bogus hatch or fish swirl and flipped me off. Concerned now about Dick's safety, I shrugged off the insult and, careful not to startle the beast, frantically gestured for Dick to look to his right. When he finally did, his jaw dropped open, his cigarette fell to the ground, and the 58-year-old cantankerous former athlete did a standing broad jump that would have made Carl Lewis proud. I doubled over in stitches, about to be carried downstream by the currents… a precursor of things to come.

Later that evening, Sausage, Shitfish and I decided to take a road trip to check out the wonders of Yellowstone. With its pristine land

and panoramic vistas, it's easy to feel the inspiration that motivated Western artists like Thomas Moran and Albert Bierstadt. Pulling off to the side of the road, we looked out from our perch on the side of a mountain, across a magnificent pastoral scene of awe-inspiring beauty. Several thousand acres of grassland, Aspen, lodge pole pines and spruce trees, rolling hills and small rivers. Sausage broke the silence by posing this question.

"Shitfish, if this were 150 years ago and you were standing here with your wife and kids trying to decide the best place to build your cabin, where would you choose?"

Shitfish pondered this question for a minute and said, "I don't know Sausage, that's a tough one."

Sausage replied, "I know where I'd choose. See that stand of trees about a mile down there on the right, just near the first bend in the river? That would be the place for me."

Shitfish became despondent and quiet. "What's wrong Shitfish?" asked Sausage.

"You picked the best damn spot."

There is an old aphorism that goes something like, "Behold the fisherman that drowned himself on expectations of fish aplenty," or maybe the original had something to do with farmers and crops, but you get the point. The Yellowstone fishing experience could only be described as frustrating and disappointing. While not disguising this emotion, Sausage was perfectly willing to apply the cliché, "Water under the bridge." Dick, on the other hand, assumed the mantle of complete responsibility for the fishing fiasco and was on edge, lashing out with a "fuck you" at the slightest provocation or perceived insult. Sausage tried to pacify Dick by assuring him that yes, you did fuck up by bringing us out here in the springtime and on opening day no less, but surely our luck will change on the Big Horn and thereby salvage the trip. Dick and Rick endorsed this sentiment whole heartedly having both experienced tremendous success on previous trips to this river.

The camp where we had reservations was located approximately a mile or two from the river in the middle of a Crow Indian Reservation. The campground itself was an amalgamation of every conceivable manner and form of camping that people could invent in an attempt to keep their heads dry and their skin insect free. Pup tents, family size tents, giant mobile homes, pickup trucks with cabs, Wally Byam Airstreams, and hippie vans were strewn across the hundred designated acres. There were a few cabins for renting (one, that would have been perfect for our motley group, included three bedrooms and a porch) where Dick had stayed on previous trips and raved about its amenities. Of course we were too late to reserve it. Our accommodations were quite different, right out of the National Lampoon Vacation genre. Two old, dilapidated school buses had been converted to sort of makeshift mobile homes, placed on cinder blocks, and rented out for $60.00 a night. Four bunk beds, the size you would find on a submarine, a tiny kitchenette and table monopolized the precious space. We stored our gear and headed out for some early evening fishing on the Big Horn.

Dick busied himself tying tippets on the lines of Sausages and me, a job he reluctantly acceded to the entire trip. Besides picking the right fly, this operation is the second most technical requirement of fly fishing. Well, besides choosing fertile fish waters. Cosmos had learned to tie his own tippets, Rick was a master, and Shitfish planned to use what was already on his 1955 Zebco Deluxe combination Spin/Fly Rod Special. Again, on the advice of shop owners and fellow anglers, we stocked up on Sow Bugs, an incredible coincidence considering that of the hundreds of possible lures the trout would still be biting these. Then we were told the devastating news. The annual spring release of water from the dam at the Big Horn head waters was happening over the next few days. We would have to fish below the surface with lead weights on our flies! Sausage had only to say,"Diiiickkkk!" to articulate his great consternation.

"But Sausage," Dick pathetically pleaded to garner the sympathy vote, "I didn't know. I've never been out here at this time of year. I have arthritis. Did I mention my dog died? Please."

The Big Horn was running at a tremendous rate, so fast that it required wading in smaller tributaries from the main body. I waded out until the water licked the top of my bib rubber suit and hooked into a monster brown trout. Keeping the rod tip high, applying steady pressure, I backed up to shallower water. However, in typical Big Blue fashion, I had forgotten my net on the shore and had to rely on Dick to assist in the landing.

Sausage and Dick were mighty impressed by my catch measuring 23 inches and an estimated 5 lbs. Sausage wanted to keep and eat the fish while Dick appealed to my "sporting" sensibilities by saying it was a "breeder" and a real sportsman would release it. I acquiesced to the latter and let it go.

I wanted to celebrate with a cold beer and a smoke … immediately. Once again, casting caution to the wind, I proceeded towards shore, high stepping and full of cheer. I lost my footing on a slippery rock and began floating down stream … rod held high out of the water. As I drifted past my Big Blue brothers, my pathetic croaks for "Help" were met with guffaws and belly laughs. Somehow, I managed to secure my footing before being swept into the main body of the Big Horn and down river to Wyoming.

The only skill involved in pitching lead is setting the hook and, in the rare event of actually hooking a fish, applying steady, constant pressure as you guide it into the net. Most of us did not have the opportunity to apply these techniques very often with the notable exception of Cosmos. He always approached life from his own independent perspective. While the fly shop owners and fishing guides all recommended "hot" flies to use, these experts also suggested a specific tippet weight. Cosmos went his own way, per usual, with regard to the tippet and this was the key to his success.

Sausage was skunked, I caught another, Dick and Rick both landed a few rainbows and brownies and Shitfish caught, well, several shitfish. Credit where credit is due however, they were not your run of the mill shitfish. Instead, these bottom feeding sucker fish weighed 3-4 lbs., and when seeing them lined up in neat little rows on the riverbank, I remarked, "They're beauties Shitfish. I only wish Maypo could be here to clean and fillet them." Shitfish nodded in solemn agreement.

Early the next day, Dick, Cosmos and I saw a promising little area to try our luck. In a rented float boat, we rowed to the edge of the shore and Cosmos hopped out to secure the anchor line to a tree limb. As he was wading to the stern, his hip caught the tip of Dick's $350 Orvis Special fly rod and snapped it off. Crestfallen, Dick reacted philosophically. "Shit happens." Cosmos offered to jog back to our "Bus Stop," a good two miles away, and retrieve Dick's spare rod. Dick did not protest and Cosmos took off. In a gesture of unparalleled generosity, I offered Dick my last beer from the small cooler that had permanently attached itself to my wrist.

The water receded with each passing hour. By the afternoon on our last day, top water fly fishing was now possible. Dick and Rick knocked 'em dead. Cosmos caught a couple of nice rainbows and cleaned them by the shoreline. He took the several pounds of trout fillets, wrapped them in foil and a freezer bag, and handed the whole package to me, "If you really are Maypo's friend, you'll put these fish in your cooler and take them back to Rhode Island for him." I pondered the thought of carrying the fish through airports, on planes and in cars and decided... of course! Maypo's my best friend and Big Blue brother known for his prosaic tastes in edible fish.

In the meantime, Sausage reluctantly retired from active participation and sat on a boulder smoking a cigarette. Although he saw a lot of activity on the surface of the water and witnessed Dick and Rick pull one trout out after another, his arms were too tired to make even one more cast. He conservatively estimated that he had "thrown lead" about 1500 times over the two days and resigned himself to the status of "skunked on the Big Horn."

The trip ended on a rather low keynote. Sausage's bursitis was very much aggravated and he was exasperated with Dick for not having researched the conditions more thoroughly. He was also annoyed with himself for trusting Dick's dubious judgment. Shitfish displayed no unusual signs of dissatisfaction, except an increased capacity to drone on about his many physical ailments and rotten fishing luck. Cosmos, Dick and I were tired and cranky. At one point, during an airport terminal connection, Cosmos' imperious nature got the best of him when he went outside to where Dick and I were having a smoke and ordered us back in NOW because the bags had arrived.

I retorted, "Hey Cosmos, I don't even let my wife talk to me like that!"

This assertion was not true of course but it drew a "Hardy Ha Ha" from Dick and just an exasperated gesture from Cosmos as he stormed away. Rick seemed to be the only one who had completely enjoyed himself. He said, "I got to catch trout in the beautiful wilds; at night, I had a roof over my head and in the morning, I had butter for my toast. What could be better than that?" Rick was right of course - the Society ethos.

A man who is able to laugh at himself will always be amused.

SENECA

ALLIGATOR

I hosted what was supposed to be a game dinner in fall of 1996. Bob couldn't come because he was recovering from colon cancer surgery. True to form, he was back on the links 6 months later trimming his handicap. **Sausage takes us away here** about the night we tried to eat the kind of reptile that nearly ate Bobby.

IT WAS WONDERFUL to see the Bobman again. He had recently completed extensive chemotherapy and looked great. He had lost a lot of weight, but his color was good, and his smile was wider than I had ever seen. We played 36 holes for four days straight and Bob played exceptional golf. I was thrilled for him and proud of him.

On the fifth day, however, things changed. The swaggering, gregarious Bob who had confidently boomed two hundred and seventy-yard drives and calmly stroked birdie putts, fell completely apart. Fatigue caught up with him. Instead of the short grass in the middle of the fairway, Bob's balls would arch way left or way right. The first sound after the ball leaving the tee was usually a profanity from Bob or the thunk of the ball hitting a tree or the swish of his club being thrown in the air. Sometimes all three sounds would occur simultaneously.

Bob lapsed into silence. He was a seething stew of emotion. Finally on the fifth hole, a long par five bordered by water its entire length, Bob launched his more typical drive. It arched high in the sky and seemed to wink at the sun before finally falling into the right center of the fairway about three hundred yards away. Bob seemed to draw strength from that shot. There was a renewed spring in his step as he strode to the cart. Perhaps he was thinking that it was not too late to salvage his round. Upon reaching his ball he reached for his driver. He would attempt to reach the green in two. Bob set up and took an unusually big swing. Two things happened simultaneously. The ball went sideways, narrowly missing his partner and his club head detached from the shaft. It bounced crazily off the fairway, end over end, ricocheted through the rough and plopped into the water. I watched the blood rush into Bob's face, but outwardly he remained calm. He walked to his cart, took his seat and motioned for his partner to go in the direction of his club head. I pulled up in my cart just as he was leaning over the bank in an attempt to retrieve the floating club head with the naked shaft.

At that moment, a large alligator swirled only a few feet from Bob. I hadn't seen Bob move that quickly since his pre-war days on the basketball court. He stumbled up the bank and loped into the safety of the fairway. He bent at the waist, still holding the golf shaft, and inhaled deeply several times. Suddenly, he pointed at the sky like Moses trying to bring forth water from the rock with his staff.

"That's fucking it!" he shouted. "I've been shot, stabbed, and stepped on a bomb! I've been in 2 car wrecks and have 5 feet of scars! I've fuckin' cancer and I'm gonna die, but I will *not* be eaten by a fuckin' reptile!"

Bob stood poised for a few seconds as if waiting for a rebuke from The Almighty. Slowly he lowered his hand, returned to his cart and didn't move from it for the rest of the round.

It was ironic that the 'gator had seemingly targeted Bob, who in many ways embodied the heart and soul of the Big Blue Society. Perhaps it was only chance, but something deep in my subconscious mind suggested something more sinister. Here was a fuckin' 'gator trying to eat Bob. I think now that the reptile acted in reprisal. I believe it was an attempt to fulfill a curse because members of the Society attempted to eat a reptile. Bob wasn't even there that night. Therein lay the irony.

The idea for an alligator dinner was spawned in the summer of 1992. Once a year, my father-in-law would travel up from Florida to spend a week with us. During cocktail hour, once properly lubricated, we would compare notes on various recipes. The topic of game dinners would invariably come up. Members of the Big Blue Society were intimately familiar with impressive game dinners. Annually, they were held at an upscale club. We had sampled elk, lion, beaver, ostrich, bear, possum, squirrel and raccoon in the past. We had discovered an appetite for creatures usually observed on episodes of the "Wild Kingdom" or lying dead in the middle of a busy highway. Although alligator was fairly common fare in parts of Florida and Louisiana, we had never tried it.

Big Al, my father-in-law, informed me that 'gators inhabited practically every body of freshwater in his part of Florida. He promised to send me some.

Several months later, without prior notice, a package arrived by UPS. Inside was a styrofoam cooler packed with dry ice and about ten pounds of a glistening, grayish-white, frozen slab of what I assumed could only be alligator.

I stored it in the freezer in my garage. Later that day, I called Maypo and suggested the Blues get together for an alligator feast. Although by brothers Cosmos and Maypo were capable in the kitchen, I had become the unofficial Big Blue Gourmand. It was more by default than anything else. Buck was good with burgers, hot dogs and steak, but not much else. Bobby had mastered Texas barbecue and eggplant parmesan, but he was after all, in Texas. Lyle, although imminently well prepared to cook a meal, usually managed to hurt himself in the process. His meals always seemed to look more appetizing before rather than after they were cooked. So, that left me. In the past, I had been successful with antelope, venison and even caribou. What could be so difficult about alligator?

In retrospect, it was my culinary arrogance that played a large part in this memorable repast. I had not consulted with Big Al about how to prepare 'gator. He said it tastes a lot like chicken or veal.

We had arranged a one-night Rendezvous at Maypo's cottage at the lake on a Friday evening in early fall. I figured that if 'gator tasted a lot like chicken or veal then I would prepare it in similar fashion. As I cut open the plastic bag containing the slab of 'gator, I was struck by the absence of markings on the package. There was no print to tell me that this cut of prime 'gator tenderloin had come from a 'gator farm. The plastic pouch was sealed with a twist tie. It was not vacuum sealed. A vision flashed in my mind of Big Al, with a high-powered rifle, a flashlight and a net on a moonless night. I pictured him perched in the bow of a dinghy, deep in a swamp with only a pair of red eyes for company. I dismissed the thought.

I carved one inch thick slabs of 'gator, sprinkled them liberally with salt and pepper and dry-rubbed it into the meat. The meat was tough but I was undaunted. Many cuts of game were tough. The key was to marinate it, break down the fibers and sinew, slow cook it and render it fork-tender. I used vinegar, white wine, water, onions, bay leaf and various herbs for the marinade. If four hours would tenderize beef, imagine what four days could do to even the toughest cut of 'gator.

We gathered at Maypo's cottage. I had managed to spill a bit of the marinade on the carpet of my car on the ride up. At first, I wasn't aware of the spillage, but gradually I smelled something different. It might best be described as floral in essence, yet not the bright, nose-tingling, multifaceted aroma of a bunch of fresh flowers. This was more the scent one gets when flowers have stayed too long in the vase. It still hints at what it once was, but there is now the stark realization that this could be something else entirely different.

I was greeted at the door by Lyle and another cousin, Didymus, a loner genius who took solace in the Big Blue. In fact, we were the only social invites he accepted.

"That looks great," Lyle opined as I walked through the door.

"Lyle, it's just a pan covered with foil. There's nothing to see."

"I know, but what I mean is I've kind of been looking forward to this all week."

Didymus lifted the foil and peered at the contents. He took a cautious sniff and said, "Wow, that is pungent."

"That's because he marinated it in Bobby's armpit all week." Maypo said.

Shitfish poked at the 'gator with the tip of his pocketknife. "How you plan on cookin' it?" he asked.

"I thought I'd grill it, " I responded.

We settled onto Maypo's deck with cocktails and cigars. Didymus was content with his Parliaments and Shitfish refused a five-dollar cigar for a Parodi. It seemed like all he ever did with those things was light them. They never stayed lit for long. We settled into the reverie of the Blues at rest. Good company, a cocktail and a cigar. Lyle lit a joint, passed it to Maypo, and propped his feet up. Maypo took a toke and inspected the joint.

"Lyle, after almost twenty-five years, you still roll a lousy joint."

"Why? What's wrong with it?"

"It's too fuckin' tight," Maypo informed him.

Lyle shook his head and leaned back. It seemed to be a periodic ritual with Lyle and Maypo. Maypo loved to needle Lyle. Lyle, despite having heard the same complaint endlessly, still responded with the same indignity as he had the first time.

Within an hour the grill was ready. Maypo had made a salad.

Shitfish had brought some wine. Didymus had stopped for bread and Lyle had managed to bring himself.

We gathered around the grill and I deposited the 'gator cutlets on the coals. Shitfish had returned from the bathroom, walked onto the deck and asked, " What's that strange smell?"

"It's our dinner," Lyle answered with raised eyebrows and a comical smile.

"Fuck you, Lyle," I said.

Didymus and cutlets

The 'gator meat really didn't look all that bad. If one didn't know it was 'gator, he easily might assume it was chicken. I managed to cut into a piece to see if it was done. I thought -wow- this is *not* the tenderest cut of meat. I removed the meat from the grill and we retired to the kitchen. We took our seats at the table and served ourselves.

For several minutes there was no conversation. We might as well have been hunched over computer terminals attempting to decipher a code. Instead, all of our energy and concentration were consumed by the 'gator medallions on our plate. They were exceedingly hard to cut. Shitfish, in classic understatement, finally asked, "Do you guys find these a wee bit tough?"

In response, Didymus put down his steak knife and opened the saw blade on his Swiss Army knife. Maypo got up from the table and returned with a nine-inch serrated blade.

"Do you have an ax?" Lyle asked.

"Fuck you, Lyle," I responded.

After several frustrated attempts with the knife, Maypo picked up a piece of 'gator and attempted to separate a bite using his teeth. Quickly, the rest of us followed his example. It worked. I had new respect for the power of the human jaw.

"Did you know that the human jaw is capable of exerting more than two hundred pounds of pressure per square inch?" Lyle asked.

"Fuck you, Lyle," I said, trying to chew a bite of 'gator.

Now that was the real problem. The stuff was as tough as an old boot. The more I chewed it, the bigger it seemed to grow in my mouth. The others were experiencing the same difficulty. It was impossible to swallow. Didymus removed a grayish-white piece of flesh from his mouth after a solid minute of steady mastication. He deposited it in his napkin and placed his rolled-up napkin on his plate, signaling that he was finished with dinner.

Didymus would find just the right words to reflect on a situation. This time was no different. Didymus pushed his chair a few inches away from the table, placed his hands behind his head and started to laugh. At first, it was just a chuckle, but soon it was a deep, uncontrollable belly laugh. Within seconds, we were all laughing. It was contagious.

Eventually, Lyle said, "That shit is awful!"

"Fuck you, Lyle." I managed to say between spasms of laughter.

It was moments such as this that served as both the catalyst and the stage for members of the Big Blue Society to demonstrate their versatility and creativity. Maypo rose suddenly from the table, opened a kitchen drawer, grabbed a hammer and nail and spiked a piece of 'gator to an exposed beam. He returned to the drawer, selected several darts and let fly. Two found the wall, but one buried to the hilt in the center of the 'gator cutlet.

Members of the Big Blue were naturally competitive. All had played sports in high school and some in college. It didn't matter if it was horseshoes, tennis, basketball, cards or dick size. If there was the inkling of a contest, the Blues approached it with gusto.

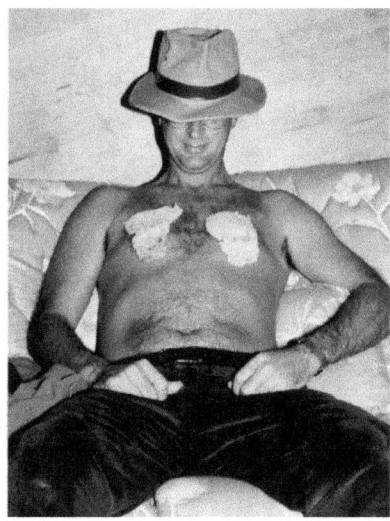

Gator Bra

Having observed Maypo's lack of respect for my meal, I joined him without hesitation. I tore off my shirt, grabbed two charred medallions and positioned them on my chest as an impromptu improvisation of a brassiere.

"It beats the shit out of edible underwear," Shitfish dead panned, igniting a new rash of laughter.

"How about using these things on cars for five mile-per-hour bumpers?" Lyle suggested.

"Fuck you, Lyle," Maypo said, mimicking me.

The evening had degenerated into a kind of culinary carnival ride. It became the Big Blue version of the movable feast. Didymus hoisted a piece of gator and attempted to ignite it with his lighter.

"I guess I was just thinking if there was another energy crisis," he explained.

Shitfish snatched a piece off the platter and attempted to cut it with a hacksaw. I flipped off my ball cap and planted a piece on my bald pate. The laughter came in rolls and racked us in fits. We held our sides and gasped for breath. I have never laughed that hard at a Blue event except for the time that an inebriated Lyle attempted to cook a steak and Bob managed to fall in the fire twice.

All the while, Maypo snapped pictures. It was the artist in him, married to the Boy Scout. His camera and a note pad seemed to be his Swiss Army knife. That camera always seemed to magically appear at the least flattering times. Maypo's words came back to me, "I have pictures."

Those words, reminiscent of the gumshoe genre, were operative in Maypo motus-operandi. If he ever decided to blackmail his fellow Big Blue members, thousands in hush money would pour into his bank account from all of the other members, except Bobby. With Bob, the plain fact of the matter was that no matter how depraved, inebriated, stoned or in what manner of frolic with small animals he appeared in Maypo's pictures, he simply didn't give a shit.

So, while Maypo snapped away, we acted out all of the possible uses for 'gator that we could imagine. Eventually, the laughter subsided. The evening was turning in upon itself. The Blues had shot their load once again. We were spent. While we were cleaning up, Lyle called from the bathroom, summoning us. We moved to the bathroom as a group. Lyle was sitting on the toilet, bare-assed with his pants around his ankles. He clutched a slab of reptile in his right hand in place of tissue. Lyle had a way with punctuation, since he had been an English major. That evening, he properly placed the exclamation point on a mini Rendezvous.

"Fuck you, Lyle," I said as I left the bathroom.

We feel and know that we are eternal.

BARUCH SPINOZA

EL WHIPPO

WE LOST OUR first man on April Fool's Day, 1999. Dr. El Whippo was called to the great Symposium in the sky. The funeral parlor was decked out in white roses, except for a floral arrangement sent by the Society. It was white carnations in the shape of fish lavished with a blue satin ribbon that bore the inscription, "Walk with God, My Friend."

I knelt by the coffin and something was off. Whippo looked too formal for a guy who spent most of his life in army fatigues and pit-stained t-shirts. He was wearing a suit, his glasses were off, his lips a tight line, his expression serene and vacant. Whippo was never like that. He always had something to say, palatable or not. I wanted him to bolt upright and flip us off, but our friend was gone. I had a Big Blue ballcap with me and fought the urge to put it on Whippo's head. Instead, I tucked it in beside him so he'd have it on the other side.

Fresh Meat asked us to be pall bearers; he said the Big Blue meant a lot to his father. The funeral was held at the college chapel and it was standing room only. We carried the casket up a flight of stairs and Whippo shifted inside. He would have laughed had we dropped him, but we caught the weight and moved on.

Whippo's coffin was set before the altar and draped with a cloth embroidered with the names of colleagues who had gone before. This was the other side of Whippo's life, his career as a teacher. A woman sang the sweetest arias I have ever heard, and there were tears. I looked out over the crowded chapel and imagined that Whippo was in the back row of the balcony, puffing a cigar like Red Auerbach.

We planted Whippo on a hilltop overlooking the Swansicut Reservoir. Pines gave way to oaks and maples surrounding the water. I stood with Fresh Meat, and he looked back at the long line of cars streaming into the cemetery.

"That's impressive," he said. "My dad came into the world with nothing and look at what he left behind."

"Yeah, us."

I heard Whippo scold me at that point. "Don't be an emotional slob, Maypo," he said. "Tell the story."

Lured Away
Dr. El Whippo
December 30, 1942 – April 1, 1999

So we did.

Don't flatter yourself that friendship authorizes you
to say disagreeable things to your intimates.

Oliver Wendell Holmes

Lyle's Rules

Lyle and I sat on my deck and discussed the logistics of the upcoming trip to Saranac. Everyone was packing a tent and a cooler except Bobby. He was free loading on Sausage as always. Once again, they were drafting charges against Lyle on, as Bobby put it, "general principle."

"We've lost our way," Lyle said. "There was a time when charges meant something. Now it's caprice and bluster. We need to define offenses and consequences."

"Amend Bobby's Rules?" I asked.

"Tweak them," Lyle said.

A few days later, these "tweaks" were in my mailbox.

AMENDMENTS TO BOBBY'S RULES OF ORDER

<u>Article 6 - Charges</u>

Any member, at any time may be brought up on charges. The member bringing the charges must have the motion seconded. Upon obtaining a second to the motion, a formal hearing will be conducted at the next society meeting. At that time, in full council, the aggrieved member will be asked to describe in detail, the alleged offense or offenses.

The member being charged will then have the opportunity to defend himself. This may or may not include witnesses and/or character references. At the conclusion of said procedure, the society will take an immediate vote on the matter. Guilty or Innocent. Yea or Nay.

Section 1 - Consequences of Action

Should the accused member be found innocent of the charges, his accuser must issue a sincere apology in front of the full society. Should the accused member be found guilty of the charge/charges, several actions are available, to be enacted by a simple majority vote:

1. Public censure

2. Loss of voting privileges

3. Expulsion from the society should the offense be egregious (requires a unanimous decision)

Article 7 - CHARGE LIST

Section 1: Breach of Society Etiquette/Conduct Unbecoming

1. Defiling campsite… (example: spilling corn or leaving other garbage strewn around)

2. Shooting pellet through a member's can of beer
   (charge more serious if member is holding said can)

3. Shooting pellet into occupied outhouse

4. Knocking a fish off another member's hook

5. Knocking another member's food off the grill and into the fire

6. Sleeping in the afternoon for more than 90 minutes

7. Absconding any community reading / visual material for one's personnel gratification (charges become more serious if material is rendered unviewable)

8. Refusal to share fishing intelligence in a timely fashion (i.e. "honey holes," lures, or techniques)

9. Compromising another member's pursuit of happiness

10. Adjusting, poking, rearranging, maneuvering or otherwise messing with a perfectly good fire

11. "Bogarting" or mongering when weed supplies are imperiled

Section 2: Ineptitude / Negligence

1. Failing to secure boat after being the last man out (charges become more serious if boat is lost)

2. Capsizing a canoe

3. Losing a paddle

4. Losing a horseshoe

5. Starting a forest fire

6. Assuming cigarette packs are empty and tossing them into the fire

7. Forgetting a fishing pole, tent, tent poles, sleeping bag etc.

8. Arriving with depleted tackle box

9. Arriving with understocked cooler

Section 3: Disregard and/or Contempt for Society Spirit

1. Excessive indulgence of hangovers

2. Excessive sleeping (see Section 1, art. 7)

3. Excessive whining and complaining

4. Early departure for capricious reasons
   (an especially egregious offense)

Lyle in his element

I come here to find myself. It is so easy to get lost in the world.

John Borroughs

The Last Campout

I PULLED INTO MY driveway with Lamar and Bobby was sitting on my front steps. He was flanked by a small travel bag and a carton of Marlboros. He rose to greet me and I saw that he had gained back most of weight he lost to chemo. He lifted me off the ground in a bear hug and kissed my neck. I was embarrassed by his show of affection in front of Lamar, but that was the Bobman.

We had dinner, Lamar went to bed, and I pulled out Lyle's Amendment to Bobby's Rules. Bob reviewed the document quickly and took offense at the idea that someone could lose their voting privileges.

"This is serious. If a guy can't vote, he can't defend himself."

"You think he went too far?" I asked.

"There are enough rules as it is. We go to get away from rules. Besides, who the fuck is Lyle to draw up charges? That motherfucker's been charged more than anyone else."

"He thinks they're meaningless without a consequence."

"Fuck the consequence," Bob said, "the charge is everything. I'm going to charge Lyle's ass for drafting this pile of shit."

Already in Big Blue mode, we stayed up late and by the time we went to bed it was nearly dawn. Bob and I loaded our gear into my

Pathfinder and strapped a fiberglass canoe to the roof. Lyle arrived and began unloading large cardboard boxes that he had packed well in advance. There was one problem with the boxes: they didn't fit in the SUV.

"You have to break some of that shit down," Bob said.

Lyle's face screwed up like we were fucking with him. He tried to cram one of the boxes in the Pathfinder and gave up. He had worked so hard to keep his stuff orderly and dry. Now, his plan was in shambles. He stood for long, lost moments pondering tent, cookstove and gear before stuffing it in the SUV. It was not how he pictured it at all.

Lamar came out with his fishing pole and school backpack. He made a last-ditch effort to come along, but I told him the day would come. I picked him off the ground and kissed his neck like Bob did me. That was our thing from then on.

My mom came to stay with Lamar, and she had a warm send-off with Bob. The dreams she had for him in terms of family and stability had come true. She was very proud. Bob melted in her embrace, the little kid again who meant good but couldn't stay out of trouble. The wildest colts....

In this chapter we trade the lead back and forth the way bluegrass musicians share single microphone on stage. **Sausage kicks it off** about our last fishing trip where the signs of age were upon us.

I stood in the shower and scrubbed. I watched the water froth brown as it churned down the drain. When I thought I was clean, I repeated the whole procedure a second time. Beneath my fingernails the dirt was caked. I imagined an autopsy. The death report would focus on fingernail findings. The coroner would be puzzled.

"As best we could make out, your husband died an unnatural death. We don't actually know what caused it. Under his nails we found ketchup, charcoal, common dirt, mustard, fish blood and trace elements of seventeen different types of alcohol, and let's not forget cannabis."

A short while earlier, Buck, Bobby and I had completed the 6 hour return trip from Saranac and Site 45. I had deposited a weary, depleted Bobby on Maypo's doorstep. Maypo, Lyle and Cosmos were about a half hour behind us. Maypo reported finding Bobby sound asleep on his back step.

"He reminded me of my dog," Maypo told me the next day. "Occasionally he disappears. When he returns, he sleeps on the back step for three or four days because he's so beat to shit. I have no idea where he goes, but it takes a lot out of him."

On the drive home I felt the five-day bristle on my chin. I contemplated growing a beard. I had grown one about fifteen years earlier. It was full and a healthy reddish-brown. A woman had remarked that it made me look ascetic. I mistakenly took it as a compliment.

Prior to the shower, I peeled off my clothes. I contemplated burning them as I observed them in a heap on the bathroom floor. For the moment, I was content to open the second story window and toss them out onto the lawn. I couldn't bear to have them close to me any longer. On the third night of the trip, I removed my sneakers to sleep. In the morning, the stench in my tent woke me! I thought a small animal had died in my tent. It was my feet.

I turned my attention to my image in the mirror. Like most men, I seldom studied my image. Women, on the other hand, are intimate with their faces. They know every blemish. They rue each tendril of the crow's feet that attack the borders of their eye sockets. Images of dried fruit and collapsed balloons haunt their dreams.

In the past, when I looked in the mirror, I would see myself in a detached sort of way. I was not aware of the changes. It was sufficient to know I was still there each morning. But now, I studied my face. My five-day growth was not a healthy reddish-brown. It was battleship gray, going to white. There were a few remnants of dark bristle like forgotten pockets of green in an otherwise parched lawn. Age lines migrated from the corners of my mouth and threatened to intersect with the growing crevice that ran between my lower lip and chin. My face, I thought as I shaved, is now a metaphor for the whole society.

On the day after we returned from Saranac, my wife and I hosted a college graduation party for my middle daughter. Among the ninety guests were Buck, Cosmos and Maypo. A still sleeping Bobby had been shipped back to Texas.

My fellow Blues were clean, neatly attired, somber and reflective. I asked Cosmos his thoughts on the trip.

"It wasn't great," he responded with typical candor.

I probed.

"The ride was too long. The weather was poor and there was too much smoke."

I recalled Cosmos leaving the lean-to when Buck lit a cigarette. A short while later, Cosmos lit a cigar and smoked with impunity.

On Monday, back at work, Bob called.

"I had a tremendous time," he related. "I loved it, but you know, Sausage, I'm not sure I could do it again."

"You mean, not right away?" I goaded him.

"I mean probably never again," he said. "You see, my body is 50, but with all that it has been through, it thinks it's 70."

"What do you think?" I asked him.

"Me?" he laughed. "I think the motherfucker's more like 80!"

Later that morning, Buck stopped in my office. We discussed the various reactions.

"Perhaps," Buck offered, "we've outgrown it."

During my 30s, I collected sports cars, 7 or 8 of them, all expensive and recklessly fast. In my 40s, I divested myself of them and now drive a sport utility vehicle. The clincher is, it's a Lexus.

Was something happening to the Society? Obviously we were

changing and aging, but I thought it would be more gradual. Bodies transform from the late thirties to the forties. I thought of my twelve-year-old Golden Retriever. He had been charged with energy and a zest for life. When he was seven, cutting figure eights in the yard, he had ruptured his anterior cruciate ligament. We had it surgically repaired for thirteen hundred dollars, but the dog was never the same. He had brushed against his own mortality. I watched his muzzle turn white almost overnight. Arthritis settled in the hip joint and he walked where he used to run. He slept most of the time.

When I was 35, on a whim, I called several longtime friends. The plan was to attempt to relive a day from the summer of our youth. We slept late, packed a cooler and set off. We played several pick-up games of basketball and downed a few beers at midday. We retired to the old swimming hole for a few forays off the rope swing. We ended up at the A & W Root Beer stand in midafternoon. The carhops looked to be the same age as my daughter. I was home in the house by four in the afternoon.

In retrospect, there were signs. I recall Buck a week before the trip. He handed me a list ranging from underwear to Kleenex. Nothing was left to chance. I studied the list and remarked to the effect that he was planning rather meticulously. He'd shrugged in response.

"We need a boat, "he said.

"We have a boat," I reminded him.

"Not big enough or fast enough," he said.

His mind was made up. He purchased a sixteen-foot runabout and powered it with a forty horsepower Mercury. In the space of two days, he registered the boat and the trailer. He outfitted it with chairs and an anchor.

"It will seat six comfortably," he informed me. He emphasized the word 'comfortably.'

"Wow!" I remarked. "I think the Society is getting rather cushy in old age."

At precisely 5:40 a.m. on a Monday morning, Buck attempted

to hook the trailer to my vehicle. The boat was carefully packed with all of Buck's stuff. The degree of planning leading up to this moment would have rivaled the space shuttle launch. Our rocket, however, threatened to fizzle. Despite our planning, things were going wrong. The wiring harness was too short. Buck stripped the wire and relocated the ground. The standard trailer lock wouldn't fit the standard hole. Buck drilled it. We were ten minutes late to meet the others and frazzled. There was a time we would have laughed about it.

A week earlier I had discussed the upcoming Rendezvous with Ralph, the proprietor of the Creamery where we were to meet our fellow Blues. Ralph was stocky with mischievous blue eyes and a fair complexion. In the mornings when I would start the day with one of his homemade muffins and a strong cup of coffee, he would vie with my newspaper for my attention. He chatted with everyone who walked in the door and considered it his mission in life to be of some assistance.

Ralph wanted to know all about our trip – Where are you going? Are you sleeping in tents? Tell me about the guys. I sensed he wanted to go and would have jumped at the chance. He would not have fit in, as evidenced by his behavior on the morning of our departure.

When Buck and I arrived, Ralph was sitting next to Bobby, staring up at him like a little kid with a cool new toy. He had asked me a week earlier if we needed any coffee. I had learned from past experience that it was important not to refuse Ralph's kindness because it obviously hurt his feelings. I had mumbled something about perhaps needing a little coffee. I no sooner sat down then Ralph presented me with four pounds of coffee and a bill for thirty dollars.

"That's a lot of coffee," Maypo observed.

I knew my fellow Blues well enough to interpret their collective glances – "Who the fuck is this guy?"

Once outside, we were anxious to be on our way. Bobby transferred to the back of my vehicle and arranged himself amidst the duffel bags.

"Is this my shit?" he asked.

True to form, Bob brought only himself. He relied on me to supply him with a tent, air mattress, sleeping bag and fishing pole. Every Rendezvous, I would purchase these items anew. For some reason, they seemed to self-destruct over the course of four days. Bob could never figure it out.

"What color is my tent this year?" he inquired with a chuckle.

At the moment that we were about to embark, Ralph emerged from the Creamery. He was frantically waving his hands in an effort to stop us. He stuck his head in the window and breathlessly slobbered all over Buck.

"Do you guys need any of those little fire starter logs?" he inquired. "I have a bunch in my gift shop."

Buck gave me a disgusted look and Ralph retracted his head like a threatened turtle.

"Fire starter logs?!" Bob exclaimed. "Fuck no! We got two fuckin' pyromaniacs in this vehicle alone!"

As I drove off, Buck informed me that he brought a blowtorch. I recalled times on past Rendezvous when the Society was lucky to produce a few soggy matches between us.

Bobby, Buck, Cosmos and I, with the aid of Buck's boat, arrived at Site 45 within minutes of our launch. In the past, we had putted along at three miles an hour in an underpowered, leaky boat or stroked a canoe for a couple of hours in order to reach Site 45. Now we whisked across the water at more than thirty miles per hour. The boat was a thrill, but something seemed lost. Perhaps that was symptomatic of every acquiescence to technology.

When Maypo and Lyle arrived at the site, Lyle was not speaking to Maypo. Lyle had misstepped launching the canoe and plunged his sneakers into the water. Naturally, he blamed Maypo. Let's hear **Lyle's side of the story**.

᪥

In keeping with tradition, Maypo and I decided we would paddle to Site 45. The canoe had been left on the dock and our gear strewn unceremoniously about by those more anxious to stakeout choice locations to pitch their tents. That left Maypo and I to fend for ourselves.

In his typical officious manner, Maypo directed where gear should be placed and, seeing that I had taken a little initiative and put a few items in the canoe, he removed and repositioned them more to his liking. As any experienced camper knows, you do not load your canoe on the dock. You set it in the water first and then load up. Granted, I had violated this tenant and placed a few items in the canoe while it was landbound. I was anxious to get going and felt that any little endeavor to this end would put us that much closer. I was also confident that we could easily lift the canoe off the dock and plop it in the water. However, I took exception to Maypo's presumptuousness and his implied accusation of my incompetence. I became lost in my own train of resentful moodiness as we continued to load the canoe with everything we had.

Now it was time to lift the ponderous thing. As one might guess, this proved no easy task. On the count of three, we heaved ho and I swung my end towards the water. At this precise moment, Maypo decided, unilaterally I might add, that this approach was doomed to failure. I could not stop the momentum and instantaneously determined that the only way to prevent disaster was for me to jump in the water and hold the canoe up so that Maypo might drag it back to safety. I was wearing sneakers, my one good pair for the trip. Maypo was in his swimsuit and wearing river sandals. Now the question must be asked, who was more prepared to jump in the water and save our asses?

Naturally, I was pissed that he forced my heroics. What made the comedy of errors so vexing in my mind was the fact that Maypo thought it extremely funny that my sneakers were soaked. I seethed, he laughed. In retrospect, his reactions were nobler than mine as laughing always is in every aspect of life. However, at the time, my thoughts were not so lofty.

The sounds of silence prevailed on our long canoe trip. Despite Maypo's incessant prodding of, "What's wrong?" I was not dissuaded from my righteous indignation. How two people can simultaneously experience the same event and, moments later, their remembrances be so diametrically opposed will forever be mysterious. Maypo insisted that he had done nothing wrong, that the situation had not been so out-of-control as I assumed, and that the canoe could have been righted had we just pulled the thing back to the dock, etc., etc. He also marveled at our incredible stupidity and reminded me that my sneakers would, in fact, eventually dry. Then, **Sausage caught me with a spare pair.**

Lyle sulked and squished by me and began to set up his tent in a clearing. A while later I sauntered over and observed him rooting in his tent like an aggravated badger. Objects seemed to pelt the tent from the inside. I leaned against a tree and watched. Eventually, Lyle's feet, followed by his knobby ass, worked their way clear of the tent. He was still wearing his wet sneakers, but in his hand he clutched a spare, dry pair.

"You brought and extra pair?" I asked in mock disbelief.

Lyle was a bit embarrassed. "You never know when something could happen, Sausage."

He stood grinning and slung his spare sneakers over his shoulder. He reminded me of the gunslinger whose pistol is shot from his hand. When all seems lost, he resorts to the derringer hidden in his boot. Lyle grabbed a towel and headed for the ledge. He no sooner put on his spare treads than he slipped and fell in. In retrospect, Lyle's predicament reeks of irony. A younger Lyle would not have brought a spare pair of shoes. He would have dried his sneakers on a sunbaked rock and cheerfully ambled about barefoot in the interim.

A few days before the Rendezvous, Fresh Meat stopped over with pictures of his father. I had asked him for a memento that we might bury at Site 45 in memory of our fallen brother. El Whippo appeared in the pictures as we best knew him. A military bush hat sat on his head. The ties were knotted beneath his chin. He wore a clean white T-shirt with a hole on the sleeve. A cigar was clenched in his mouth and his expression was best described as a sneer.

He was in remission at the time of the photo and the sneer expressed his contempt for the disease that was trying to take him. I had planned to bury something at the site but as I unwrapped the picture inside my tent, I changed my mind. Burying Whippo had been enough. I had not been able to linger by the casket when they lowered it.

I took the picture in the silver frame and placed it on the picnic table. The bar had been reborn and El Whippo was placed in the middle of it. I stepped back. He seemed as comfortable surrounded by the bottles as a fur ball on a cat. Later, as a sign of respect when the table served as a blotter for spilled food and beverage, I moved him to the lean-to and tacked him to a beam where he could see everything a little better as **Maypo will attest.**

"A moment of silence," Sausage said, tapping his knife on the picture frame.

"To Whippo," Buck said, raising a glass of scotch bottled about the same time Lyle and I discovered Saranac.

"Grab a bottle," Bobby said. "We're toasting Whippo."

Cosmos sailed off with a Dixie cup of tequila, spilling it on his hand and licking it off. Buck nodded seriously to the empty camp chair beside him. "Whippo's right here."

We felt his presence at that moment. Bobby gassed back and told us what he thought Whippo was up to.

"He's fishing with Jesus. Now there's a guy who loved to fish. If He was here, He'd walk on water. What kind of shit is that, eh Sausage? I mean, you hang your dick out your pant leg and say, 'I'm the only guy who can do that.' But the Big Fisherman walks on water and says, 'I'm the only guy who can do that.'"

It was classic Bobby. He often combined the sacred and the profane, two sides of his nature that he brought together like a cymbal clash. He was saint and sinner, visionary and barbarian, poet and peasant, all tumbled into one incredibly strong, certifiably insane, megalith of a fat man.

That night, we ate steak. Steak is more than a piece of cow. Guys stalk their steaks in supermarkets, track them down in butcher shops and fight for them in discount clubs. Our steaks sizzle with all that it means to be a dominant male. The bigger the steak, the bigger the man and, make no mistake, size does matter.

Lyle had taken crap about his steaks in the past and was determined to rise in stature. He slapped a massive sirloin on the grill with an attitude of, "Take that." But his steak was frozen solid and refused to cook. While the rest of us dined on ribeyes and tenderloins, Lyle danced between the grill and the table, cutting into his cold slab and returning it to the fire. He ate his potato and polished off a can of corn before sitting down for a final go at his steak. A few disappointing bites and he chucked the laggard meat into the fire and settled for a hot dog. The Magic Chef was back, and seeking the highest office **according to Sausage.**

Ever since his ignominious defeat almost ten years earlier, Lyle had unabashedly sought the highest office of the Society, the Presidency. Unchastened by his loss, he hurled unflattering pundits at my presidency, which came about when Bobby was deemed unfit to serve. Several weeks before the Rendezvous, I received one of Lyle's infamous missives. In part, it read:

"Ouch! Perhaps I'm being too harsh in my critique.
I think it's time we debunk this Sausage Mystique.
You've had your reign as Presidential despot
We salute your departure with a resounding fart."

I responded in kind, an excerpt of which stated:

"It's my job you want, you lecherous fool
Well you might as well eat my presidential stool."

At one point I asked Lyle in all seriousness if being elected president was important to him. "It would be in my obituary," he said.

On the second night following a late dinner, we convened around the fire. The scene was reminiscent of so many nights on past Rendezvous but, as I glanced at my fellow Blues, something struck me as different. It took me a moment to figure it out. Site 45 was the same. Except for some recent graffiti carved into the logs of the lean-to, all seemed to be as we had left it nearly ten years earlier. The fire crackled and spit embers into the darkness. Wisps of smoke from the fire married the smoke from several cigars and drifted towards the spruce canopy above us. The light reflected off faces and glinted dully off the aluminum frames of our camp chairs.

Camp chairs, I suddenly thought. We sat collectively and contentedly ensconced in the relative luxury of camp chairs. Coolers that had served as seats on past Rendezvous had been relegated to the back of the lean-to. Camp chairs were a concession to comfort in much the same way as Buck's high-powered motorboat. My mind flashed ahead ten years and I envisioned future Rendezvous. Porches and Adirondack chairs sprung to mind. Conventional meals served by staff and perhaps a boat ride if the weather was ideal. I dismissed the thought and returned to the more pressing matter of the evening – nominations.

The question of who would be the next Grand Scrotum hovered

over the Society like an uninvited horsefly. It wasn't with the same ponderous heart-thump of a papal election, but it was nevertheless important in its own right. Nobody was more aware of that then me. I had been the Scrotum for the better part of ten years. I had indulged in all of the privileges of office. I had carried sway on Rendezvous destinations. I had taken the Society international as I had promised on my election night. I had recommended a Big Blue website that was in the process of becoming a reality. And even my dick, consistent with the presidential privilege of being able to hang it out the side of my shorts, had spent so much time in the fresh air that it seemed to protest every time I had to stuff it back in my Jockeys.

But now it was all coming to an end. I resigned my presidency on the first night of the Rendezvous. I searched the faces of my fellow Society members, knowing full well that from this August body would emerge my successor. I had spoken with Bob earlier that evening when we were fishing.

"Lyle thinks he has it in the bag," Bob said.

"What's he basing that on?" I asked.

"Well, who's left?" Bob responded. "I mean, think about it. Buck has been the Scrotum, Maypo had his chance, we're all tired of your raggedy ass, so who's left?"

"What about you, Bob?" I inquired.

"Fuck that. I won't subject myself to the abuse and lack of confidence on the part of my fellow members. I was found unfit to serve almost ten years ago." His voice softened and he continued. "I'll be damned if I'm any more fit today. So you can forget about my sorry ass."

"What about Cosmos?" I asked. "He's never been president."

"Cosmos?" He echoed. Bob seemed to be asking himself the question. "I don't fuckin' think so," he said.

"Why not?"

"Well, think about this, Saus. Cosmos takes his whole family around the world for a year. He flies into fuckin' Africa without a single reservation. I mean, he traveled for a whole year with his family. He never made any plans. When he got tired of a place, he just up and left. Quite honestly, I don't think the membership would support him."

"So-o-o," Bob continued, "in Lyle's mind, that leaves only him."

That evening my attention was drawn to Candidate Lyle snugly cosseted in his lawn chair by the fire. Consistent with the Big Blue modus operandi, to part with convention and that which reeks of the politically correct, I decided to support Lyle. In fact, I championed his causes by making an impassioned nomination speech on his behalf. It is not the easiest thing to become impassioned on Lyle's behalf. Seldom has Lyle become impassioned on his own behalf. If people were compared to toys, Lyle would not have been an "action hero." I believe he would have been a "slinky" or perhaps a "bobble-head." It's rumored that for his high school's annual dramatic presentation, rather than portray a character, Lyle was a prop.

As I spoke on his behalf, I watched Lyle from the corner of my eye. He resettled himself in his chair. He sat up straighter in an attempt to achieve a more presidential posture. The mouths of my fellow Blues were collectively agape as I extolled Brother Lyle's virtues. When I was finished, the only sounds were of the night. The crackle of the fire, the whisper of a breeze, the voice of a frog at the water's edge. I let the silence sit. The pregnant pause was exaggerated by the woodsy setting. Eventually, I asked if there were any other nominations. Only more silence greeted my request. I was disappointed because it appeared that Lyle was correct in thinking that he was a "sure thing." At the moment that I was about to declare that Lyle would run unopposed and therefore win by default, Buck changed the complexion of the election.

"I nominate Whippo," he declared, rising unsteadily from his chair.

"But… but…he's dead!" a shocked Lyle stammered, fixing Buck with a stare.

"Doesn't matter," Buck responded. "You're going to have to explain what you can do for the Society that El Whippo can't."

Lyle sank in his chair. His shoulders hunched in. The lip appeared suddenly like the moon emerging from behind a cloud. Lyle pondered the flames a few feet away.

"Fuckin' Lyle," I heard Bobby saying in the background. "You're running against a dead man and you're not doing too good."

It was to be my apotheosis, the highlight of my impending obituary, the zenith of a very subtle decade-long political campaign to answer the call. I rationalized my nomination as fate and had already practiced my speech. It was supposed to go something like this:

"I'm tired of playing the role of sycophant just to bolster the fragile egos of previous presidential despots. Tired of being the brunt of societal jokes just to impart the lesson of not taking oneself too seriously. I will lead the Society into the new millennium with my own vision of manifest destiny. We will break the shackles of restraint that have bound us to mediocrity and propriety. With my steady hand at the helm, I will steer our ship with unwavering resolve (as long as I'm not asked to carry a plate of corn after cocktail hour). Whereas under past leadership we have floundered on the sandbars of complacency and indolence, history will distinguish my presidency as one of unbridled enthusiasm, divine inspiration, and perpetual energy. The Society will enjoy a veritable cornucopia of guilt-free hedonism. I will lead by example. Vote for me!"

It was so close; I could feel the presidential scepter in my hand, my eyes dazzled by the brilliance of the presidential seal; I yearned to wag my presidential prerogative from the leg of my shorts in the time honored Big Blue salute. I couldn't wait to savor the eye-watering effects of that first presidential tequila shot. It was so close....

≈

Lyle and I, the Bobman, burned the midnight oil that night. Our happy campers fell out in exact order beginning with Cosmos as early as 6 p.m. Sausage and Buck followed like a pair of matching book ends. Maypo would hang in there a while longer and, depending on the topic of conversation, he could be a real trooper. But the fact of the matter remained, the Society went to bed earlier. We were more susceptible to the elements. We were tired, we were older. Lyle and I talked about it, actual philosophical conversations, seeking solutions to everything from extrication of the redundant prepoose to the prerogative of those creatures from Venus. We settled nothing but proved that we had changed by our ability to piece together a sentence after midnight.

Lyle had worked third shift for over ten years. He had become a nocturnal beast by way of habit and was as comfortable in the night as a prowling coon. I, on the other hand, have been an insomniac for as long as I can remember, fueled by a host of neurosis that outnumber those in the diagnostic and statistical manual. We were perfect company for each other, a couple of lunatics searching for Zen.

"Let me ask you something, Lyle. Why in the world do you want to be president of Blue?"

"It's all about respect," he answered.

I chuckled, "You know, Lyle, it's not like you get a corporate credit card. There are no perks. It's a thankless fucking job, Lyle."

"I want your respect, Bob, and I want your vote."

Well, he didn't want much. His words just rolled off his tongue like cream style corn. But as for my respect, I told him how the cow ate the cabbage.

"Look, Lyle, we come out here once a year and from the time

we arrive until the time we leave, you put on a show. You are poster child for the temperance movement. You stagger, you stumble, you trip, you speak in half sentences, you slur your words, you slurp, you slobber, you eat things that would make a varmint puke, and these are some of you better qualities. Really, Lyle, these are the things I admire most about you. So you have my respect, but I can't promise you my vote."

I might just as well fired a shot into the snow covered slopes of mount Everest. Lyle went into lip avalanche, shocked by my candor and appalled by my viscous verbal attack. Admittedly, I had my own admirable qualities, but these went without saying. And besides, you couldn't hurt my feelings if you dipped me in shit and rolled me in crackers.

I love Lyle. He's a real good sport. The truth is we were like a couple of old coons sitting off in the woods. We looked at each other with bags under our eyes, rubbed our greasy little mitts together, and plotted the kind of mischief that could only be found while 40 miles from nowhere.

"Are you tired, Lyle?"

It was more a suggestion than a question. He wasn't ready. Lyle was on a bender, and it looked good on him. Suddenly, what to my wondering eyes should appear but a tousle-headed lad in his underwear. It was Maypo. He was a man on a mission. Lyle's eyes widened, not unlike that of the cat who just spotted the canary.

"What in the hell are you doing?" Lyle asked.

Maypo was bent over in the lean-to and rummaging through the boxes of dry goods.

"I'm looking for Twinkies," he replied with a touch of frustration in his voice.

Lyle looked at me. His gaze seemed to suggest that there was a new target for our barrage of lewd insults and, reminiscent of a forward observer, Lyle dialed in the new coordinates.

"Just what do you have in mind for that Twinkie," he asked.

Maypo was suffering from selective deafness, knowing only too well that any line of questioning from the drunken likes of Lyle and the Bobman spelled double trouble.

Lyle inquired, "Is there anything in Bobby's Rules to cover the molestation of dessert foods?"

I had to get involved.

"I think he'll be okay as long as the cream filling doesn't shoot about the campsite. That would fall into the legal definition of Defiling," I added.

Maypo tucked the June issue of the North American Beaver under his arm and, with Twinkie in hand, tip-toed off to his tent. Lyle and I laughed well into the night and, before retiring, prepared a disparaging note to Maypo which we wrapped around a Twinkie and left at the edge of his tent.

Lyle and I went our separate ways. I had pitched my tent 6 feet from the shoreline of Lake Saranac on a bed of pine needles. I clearly had the best view of the channel and loved the soothing sound of the lake. I paused for a moment, taking in the silver water under a three-quarter moon. Then I saw it, what has been spoken about in the Northwoods for many years. It goes by various names and descriptions, but it is nothing less than the Saranac Lake Monster. It rose from the depths and fixed me with a penetrating stare. Then it was gone and I saw only my reflection.

On the third day, we took a boat ride. In the past, boats were a necessary means of transportation from one promising fishing spot to another. On this day, however, we had set out with the express purpose of taking a boat ride. It reminded me of my aunts and uncles when I was an adolescent. On weekends, they would gather with my family at a nearby lake. Late afternoon, they would assemble in my Uncle Joe's boat with their cocktails for a cruise of the lake. I recall shuddering inwardly with the perception of a thirteen-year-old hoping that I would never be that old. As I sat next to Cosmos in Buck's boat, in my ever-present lawn chair surrounded by the Blues, I realized with a thump that I was now that old.

We motored sedately up the narrow 2-mile river that connected Lower and Middle Saranac Lake. The water was shallow with a soft current. Driftwood in various sizes and poses dotted the shore. At one point we slowed to accommodate an approaching canoe carrying a college-age couple. I watched the young man in the stern sit up taller. He seemed to suck in his stomach and flex his shoulder and chest muscles as we approached. He reminded me of a dog whose hair rises in an effort to appear larger if he feels threatened. I tried to see us from his perception as we drew close. Alone with his girl-friend in an isolated place. Six scruffy, sunburned men in ballcaps, crowded into a boat on a weekday afternoon. We passed within several feet and exchanged greetings. He looked back several times as we widened the distance between us. His shoulders relaxed and his paddling became more rhythmic.

The day before, we had cruised lower Saranac. On past trips, hampered by canoes or underpowered boats, we had seen little of the lake. The effort had not been worth it. Consequently, Lower Saranac, for the most part, had remained a mystery. Mountains mimicked each other and points of cover looked surprisingly the same. It was easy to get lost and with that in mind we had never fished out of sight of camp in the evening. With Buck's boat, the sense of mystery and much of the charm was gone. We breezed around the lake and reached distant points in minutes. Part of me relished the past. I thought of grammar school math and life before the calculator.

New York State Archives

Tom's Rock

We stopped at the base of a steep cliff that rose more than 100 feet. We tied the boat at the base and made our way up a steep, winding trail to the summit. Bob arrived at the top wheezing and spent. Buck had assisted him most of the way. There was a small stone lean-to and the remnants of an old campfire. There was a bronze plaque affixed to the side of the lean-to. The writer in Maypo was drawn to it. He identified it as part of a Robert Service poem entitled, "A Rolling Stone. " The plaque read:

"Then here's a hail to each flaming dawn!

And here's a cheer to the night that's gone!

And may I go a roaming on

Until the day I die!"

The site was called Tom's Rock in memory of a boy who suffered poor health but loved his camping experiences on Saranac Lake. Maypo thought that the poet, Robert Service, would have been a "natural" for the Society. Wasn't that us? With our thirty years of Rendezvous, weren't we the romantic embodiment of his philosophy? We were the wanderers in the wilderness with our sense of adventure, freedom, and unflagging energy.

But reality was painting a different canvas. Lyle napped in a shady recess. Cosmos sat with his back to a tree. Maypo perched at the precipice, cranky joints beginning to acquaint themselves with the specter of arthritis. Bobby was still gathering strength for the trip down. As I rose, I heard myself grunt. When had the grunting started? Every time I stood, I grunted. When I sat, I grunted. When I shifted my weight in the chair, I grunted. "And may I go a roaming on until the day I die."

Middle Saranac was different from Lower. There were fewer islands and consequently larger expanses of water. As a result, we didn't feel that Middle Saranac exuded the charm or the mystery of Lower. We found a rocky promontory in Hungry Bay and climbed to the top. It was not quite as steep or tall as Tom's Rock, but the view was more expansive and spectacular. The outcrop was covered with bright daisies that grew in the minimal soil between cracks and crevices. They were survivors. They reminded me of Bobby, who had survived two tours of Nam, a couple car wrecks, three marriages, and a bout with cancer. Maypo picked a daisy and placed it in his notebook. We christened it "Bob's Rock," and the Bobman was truly pleased.

I picked a daisy at Bob's Rock and pressed it in my notebook as a way to remember the place, the day, the 6 of us perched up there looking out on Middle Saranac. It was similar to picking a clover at Lonesome Bay, but they meant different things.

Lonesome Bay was the start of Big Blue trips to the Adirondacks. We found it by accident, a stab in the literal dark, and the clover represented the luck of finding a place the Society would call home for over 20 years.

The daisy at Bob's Rock symbolized the end of that run. Whippo was gone, and we were losing our ability to camp. Bob never would have made it up Tom's Rock if Buck hadn't put a shoulder to his butt and pushed him up the whole way. Camping was hard on Bob, and it had lost its allure. I picked the daisy as a memento, but it would play important a role in the future of the Society.

✍

When we first visited Saranac years ago, the fishing, if not spectacular, was still good. A concentrated 3 hour effort would always produce bass and pike. We kept only what we ate and we never went without fish. We had heard that the effects of acid rain had depleted the fishing, but we didn't want to believe it. Cosmos related it to returning to the high school reunion only to find that the prettiest girl in the class had blown up like a tick. The memory would have been better.

Without the promise of fish, we abandoned the effort. More time was spent in camp. Horseshoe games were longer. Meals were prepared more leisurely. We slept later in the morning. It was Buck, however, in the absence of fishing, who introduced a new sport to the Big Blue Rendezvous: golf. Late each afternoon, armed with a cocktail, an oversized driver, a remnant of carpet, a few dozen golf balls and a buzz the size of Brooklyn, we would assemble on the ledge. Taking turns, we would drive balls in an effort to hit a granite cliff, The Devil's Pulpit, more than three hundred yards away. We seemed to collectively delight in the lunacy of it. It was typical of the Big Blue Society and that's why it felt so natural.

Several years ago, I took up golf in earnest. A friend who's a scratch golfer became my mentor. He prodded and cajoled and watched my progress. When I returned from the trip, I informed him that I had played poorly.

"What do you mean?" he had asked. "I thought this was a fishing trip?"

"It was," I informed him, "but I managed to hit some balls. The only problem was that every one of them landed in the water."

On the last night, we held elections. Lyle seemed nervous. It was probably the first time in any election that someone ran against a deceased opponent. To add insult to injury was the distinct possibility that Lyle could lose.

In past elections, I often had sensed the direction of political winds. I had felt the political pulse of my peers and knew who would capture their vote. In this election, sniff as I might, I knew nothing. I cast the first vote for Lyle. I had toyed with the idea of nominating Lyle and rooting for El Whippo, but Lyle had made a point of thanking me for my support. I couldn't let him down. I recalled the dejected figure of ten years ago, wobbling off the rock in search of solace and a place to lick his political wounds.

On the first ballot, I don't recall who voted for whom, but I do know that it came down to Bobby's vote. Bob had retreated to the picnic table and summoned me for a consultation. I did know one thing. When it came to elections, I owned Bob's vote. We both knew it. Bob was my butt boy. I controlled one third of the vote. I was no longer the president, but I was still a kingmaker and Lyle was my prodigy. Bob cast the vote in Lyle's favor and the election resulted in a tie.

On the second attempt we went to a secret ballot. Without prior knowledge, Bobby and Cosmos unexpectedly switched their votes, resulting in a second tie. Maypo withdrew the daisy from his notebook. He suggested that we settle the matter by plucking petals from the daisy. It was only fitting, considering the connection between daisies and death. Maypo handed it to me as the outgoing president and I commenced the exercise.

Lyle drew close and shuffled his feet in expectation. He reminded me of my dog who, as a puppy, had a tendency to wet himself when he became too excited. Lyle, El Whippo, Lyle, The Whip. I took my time. To my disappointment, the final petal decided the election in El Whippo's favor.

"Fuck!" Lyles exclaimed and headed for the bottle of Scotch.

"I think you have to do something," Cosmos counseled. "Split the last petal," he suggested.

I retrieved the remnant of the daisy and, in an attempt to split the petals, determined that there were indeed two. Maypo demanded to see it and was dumbfounded. He really wanted Whippo to lead. Lyle, at first, would not believe the discovery, but as the evening wore on, he concluded that El Whippo had intervened on his behalf.

"I think it's the good doctor's way of saying that I'm the best man for the job."

At my daughter's graduation party after the trip, Lyle sauntered onto the premises two hours late. He wore a muscle shirt, Big Blue ball cap and sandals. He carried a small cooler and his lip was not distended. I introduced him to my father-in-law as the president of the Big Blue Society. My father-in-law remarked to Lyle that it was a high honor to meet the president of the Society. Lyle looked him straight in the eye and shook his hand firmly.

"Indeed, it is," was all Lyle said.

We left Site 45 in the rain. Bobby packed everything in a clear plastic bag. Everything in the bag was soaking wet and covered with leaves and pine needles. He looked apologetic as he handed it to me. We exchanged a glance that spoke of an understanding between us. This was why I had to buy him new gear every time we went on a Rendezvous.

When we pulled into the boat launch area, we had to wait to haul out the boat. We exchanged greetings with two men who were launching their boat. They had driven all night from New Jersey and bristled with the same excitement that had infected us a few days earlier. Bobby assisted them with their gear. He spotted an empty beer can in the bottom of their boat.

"You guys don't plan on drinking any beer out there, do you?" he asked.

They looked confused as they searched his face for a clue.

"Well, yeah, why?" one finally managed to ask.

"Well, because they don't allow any alcohol anymore," Bob erroneously informed him.

"Shit!" one fellow said. "Well, I'll be fucked!" the other added.

Bob attempted to console them.

"At least the fishing is good."

"No kidding," they said, brightening.

"Yup," Bob said, "we killed 'em all week, just off Bob's Rock. It's on the map."

The last photo from the last campout. I ran out of film and tried to take one more photo on the roll. The sprocket holes tore, the film did not advance, but the shutter reset. Click. Bob saluting us on his way home superimposed over him and Lyle from the night before, a fitting tribute to our days at Saranac.

Buck flying

Memory is where our youth lives after it is gone.

John Cameron Swayze

Permission

WE LEFT SARANAC on a Friday morning and Buck's boys arrived the following afternoon. They camped on Green Island and had a tremendous week. Each brought a 30 pack of beer, a dozen hotdogs, cheap cigars, and their own tent. They went in on fifteen pounds of chicken wings, seven pounds of hamburger, assorted deli meats, and a case of Little Debbie snacks. As to contraband, they were tight lipped, which struck me as very Big Blue.

I managed to pry one scene from Buck's boys about what they did for six unbroken days. It seems that Woody, a hard-nosed, Division One hockey player, took a flying tour around the lake in Buck's boat. Nothing special about that, a muscled youth buzzing campsites in pooty pursuit. The difference was the long blond wig sewn into Woody's ball cap. The tresses flew out behind him like a cape as he sped down the lake.

Our lives come and go that fast. Sometimes, we wish we could relive parts of it, which is why we keep going on Rendezvous, for one more laugh, one more fire, one more chance to set the wild man free. The spirit still moves in us, just a little slower with each passing year.

The other night, Lyle, Sausage, and I fished a back cove at the Swansicut Reservoir. Sausage had not returned since he and Bobby were banned. We parked the car a safe distance away and avoided the conspicuous fishing spots. In a hide-away cove, we cast lines and ate meatball sandwiches. It was good to be back at our favorite fishing hole… until an elderly security guard came up behind us.

"Catch anything," he asked.

Sausage played it cool. "Nothing to speak of."

Lyle didn't look at the guy hoping he'd magically disappear. I noted his short stature, weak build and commanding overbite. He considered us, 3 older guys wetting a line and minding our business. We weren't the kind to break bottles or burn down the woods.

"You have permission," he said, "but leave no trace."

Sausage looked at the guy and I sensed him peeling back the layers of time to get to someone he once knew.

"Thanks," was all he said.

The guard left, and Sausage turned to us. "Can you believe that? We have fucking permission. It's come full circle."

We let it soak in for a minute or two, then Lyle lodged an objection.

"I have a problem with 'permission.' How about something more solid like 'authorized.' We're authorized to fish the Res."

Sausage didn't care what we called it, the Bobman would be psyched – our favorite fishing haunt was back on the map. Sausage started talking about taking permission to the next level: camping on one of the islands. Insert a team at nightfall, hide our canoes and campfire, stay for a long weekend. It had the ring of another Big Blue adventure where boundaries get pushed to the limit and there'd be hell to pay if we got caught.

The next day, I called Bobby who was keeping an eye on his daughter and a friend in his backyard pool. The girls were forbidden to wear bikinis because the pool was visible from the 9th hole fairway where golfers tended to hit their second shot. Bob didn't like them peering into the yard and seeing him watching little girls in little bathing suits.

"I feel like a fucking pervert," he said.

I told him Sausage's idea about camping on an island in the

Res. Lyle and I could do a scouting trip. If we got away with it, Bob would fly up and for a reservoir Rendezvous.

"Fuck that, Maypo. I'm done sleeping on the ground. I slept on the ground for 2 fucking years. I can't do it anymore. I need creature comforts."

"Like… a sofa?"

Ice cubes clinked in a tumbler.

"You ever heard of the Great Camps? You find them on lakes up north, rustic manors built at the turn of the century. Folks from Boston would travel up with staff and summer in style. That's the future of the Society, great camps."

I stopped by Sullivan Gravel and found Buck in the warehouse helping Cosmos install powerful electric motors on his sailing kayak. With its winglike outriggers and aerodynamic shape, Cosmos's boat looked like it could fly given the proper amount of thrust, and he seemed to be headed in that direction.

"Ever heard of great camps?" I asked.

Cosmos had.

"Yeah, they dot the shores of lakes like Squam. Built around the turn of the last century, set up with servant quarters, big kitchens and facilities."

"Facilities?" Buck asked.

"Tennis courts, sleeping porches, boat houses, game rooms, fire pits, gazebos. They have it all."

"I'll look into it," Buck said.

He was done with camping too. Too much stuff to bring, too many things to go wrong, too much dirt and debris in his tent. He hated climbing in and out of it on his hands and knees.

Buck did his research which was thorough as always. He weighed the pros and cons of lakes down to annual flush, health of the fishery and seasonal weather patterns. He evaluated camps in terms of size, location, views, sleeping quarters and privacy. A deciding factor was always the fire pit. The Society could not go without a fire - the pyromaniacs among us would revolt.

It was the dawn of a new age for the Big Blue. We were middle-aged men and wanted our amenities. Everyone got a bed, and Bob had his pick of sofas to sleep on. There were fridges for beer and screen rooms if the skeets attacked. Competition expanded to billiards, ping-pong and darts. Horseshoes, our mainstay, felt heavier than usual so we resorted to Extreme Bocce played on rolling terrain, gravel driveways and ungroomed trails. Power boats replaced canoes, and the fishing was legendary when we hit it right. Triple hooks-up in a boat were common in the spawn. If our timing was off, we hunted prey with fishfinders. Smallmouth tail-walked on the water, pike stared you in the face before running drag and breaking line. Camping fit our younger selves; great camps suited our aging bodies.

Our first rental was Loon Lodge, in Belgrade, Maine, only fitting for a bunch of loons. We spread out on the porch rockers, went through the bathroom window, struggled to stay upright in lawn chairs, and met with a new distraction: cable TV. Guys focused on tennis matches at Wimbledon, specifically women's matches, specifically one player's tits. TV was eliminated after that.

Horsecock and Lyle

Thus far we have rented 12 camps, in 7 states and flew puddle-jumpers to Lake Mojikit in Ontario, Canada. New blood has come into the Society in the form of Horsecock. Others wait in the wings like Lardass and Dick Shadow. They haven't been on Rendezvous yet, but the Bobman's ready. He wasn't the only one who found balance in Big Blue; I think we all did.

There is a wild man in each of us craving to break out and taste freedom. That's the legacy of the Blues, and we are not alone. Countless brother and sisterhoods cut loose and have stories to tell. Cosmos ran into one recently, the Pussy Posse. He said they were uninhibited, feral, and we should never meet up. Pooty pursuit is against the bylaws and we're after something else.

Consider this an invitation to join our ranks. Make your own rules and break any that hold you back. Adventure, explore, exit your comfort zone. Go For It. Deny Everything. Etch lines in the face of time with laughter. Go Big Blue. Long live the Society.

The End

About the Authors

Mark Cavanagh, author of *The Monocle Trilogy*, *The Zen of Laundry* and *RV Time Machine*, lives with his wife by the Ponaganset Reservoir in Chepachet, Rhode Island, where he fishes, boats, skates and skinny-dips.

Norman Hansen, a decorated war hero, wrote *Nam: A Rock Opera* and *Neptune's Reach*, a novel. He lives with his wife and daughter in League City, Texas, where Bruce golfs and volunteers at the Veterans Hospital.

Brian Cavanagh, businessman and philanthropist, wrote *The Green Boat*, a novel. He and his wife split their time between Florida and Rhode Island where they host a constant flow of children and grandchildren.

William Lally and his wife live in Scituate, Rhode Island, by the Reservoir which he patrols regularly with his fish pole and chocolate lab Odyss. William is an avid reader and enjoys extended visits with his children and grandchildren.

Shitfish, Sausage, Horsecock, Doc, Didymus,
Lyle, Maypo, Bob O, Cosmos

AFTERWORD

In New England we watch the cycle of life play out in the four seasons: rebirth of Spring, maturing of Summer, aging of Fall and dormancy of Winter. By analogy, the Society has experienced a similar transformation. We busted out on our first fishing trip, got the hang of it camping, eased into Great Camps, and now our Rendezvous days are done. More than half of the original Society members are gone: Whippo, Didymus, Shitfish, Bobby, Big Tom and Buck. We went on a few trips without them, but it was not the same. None of the antics, none of the mayhem, more sedate and, of all things, civilized. We kicked back on Golden Pond, had a few pops and reminisced. At one point, Cosmos channeled the Bobman with Sausage posing the questions. Bob's guidance was priceless. "Lip up, Lyle. Don't wuss out, Maypo. Rod tip high, Horsecock." The dead never leave who remain in our minds and hearts.

We could have written more chapters about the "slow smokeless burning" of our decay, but one scene will suffice: Bob's Belly, **written by Cosmos.**

Though we were always primed and on the lookout, we were never prepared. Bobby would just start in. The shrapnel wounds in his belly were rarely seen but those times were disquieting. Multiple deep canyons crossed over a foot of his gut. We were drawn in as to how they got there, his time in the hospital and that the guy in front of him saved Bobby's life from that Bouncing Betty. So, after supper one night and before elections, Bobby started in. He lifted his shirt and squeezed intersecting mounds this way and that such that a large, distorted mouth, or worse, appeared. It became a kind of ventriloquist dummy. With various voices, falsetto included, Bobby had us in stitches. What he said, I can't remember… and if I did; I couldn't repeat. His "scar dummy" would carry on a monolog or maybe ask rhetorical questions we were in no shape to answer. You had to be there and if you had, it wouldn't have happened. Only we had been invited to another raucous, impromptu, and sometimes obscene skit… the stuff of legends.

The first draft of this book came out 25 years ago. We passed it around, knew it needed a rewrite and shelved it to collect dust. Recently, Sausage's grandsons asked to read it, so we kicked it into shape. This is our way of putting that baby to bed.

The words Bob wrote in my notebook so many years ago ring true. "What will we do when we're too old to go on these trips? We'll make a hypnagogic return to the days of the Big Blue." This book recalls those days, a great comfort as our Winter sets in.

If you enjoyed this book, please tell a friend.

Word of mouth is the most powerful recommendation of all.

Bobby's inner child thanks you.

www.ingramcontent.com/pod-product-compliance
Lightning Source LLC
Chambersburg PA
CBHW070556130626
46556CB00001B/179